IT'S REAL MINISTRY

HOW PART-TIME AND BI-VOCATIONAL CLERGY ARE CHALLENGING AND EMPOWERING THE CHURCH

I. Ross Bartlett

Kate Jones
Research Assistant

 FriesenPress

One Printers Way
Altona, MB R0G 0B0
Canada

www.friesenpress.com

ISBN
978-1-03-915173-4 (Hardcover)
978-1-03-915172-7 (Paperback)
978-1-03-915174-1 (eBook)

1. RELIGION, CLERGY

Distributed to the trade by The Ingram Book Company

Table of Contents

Preface

What is part-time ministry and how significant is it?

This study arises from my work as Formation Director at the Atlantic School of Theology, working with students in both our on-campus and summer-distance programs. As a long-time participant in United Church Presbytery meetings, I was aware that we had been approving part-time calls and appointments for many years. Because those came in ones and twos, I did not have a clear picture of the full extent of the phenomenon within the United Church. With a little investigating, it became evident that many of our graduates would spend some or all their ministerial careers in such settings, and we were not, intentionally, doing anything to help them prepare for that reality. At the same time, Kate Jones (now ordained) presented her graduation project: a study of bi-vocational ministry and the experiences of some practitioners.

As I dug deeper, I discovered that the church, nationally, has very little data on clergy in part-time calls/appointments. While part-time and bi-vocational ministry is much more common and more fully researched in the United States and amongst (self-described) evangelical faith groups, for reasons that we will discuss below, that data does not always map well onto main-line denominations. So, with the generous support of the United Church Foundation, we set out to develop a baseline of information about part-time and bi-vocational ministry in the non-Indigenous United Church. Through surveys, interviews, and workshops, we developed some insights into this growing phenomenon and pinpointed some places where some hard choices and challenging adaptation will need to be made. After we completed our research and were writing this text, the General Council Executive received a report, "Ministry Leadership to meet the Needs of the Church in the 2020s," which will be the kickoff to a major con-versation about ministry. We hope the current study will be a useful contribution to that crucial exploration.[1]

+ + +

Many people helped bring this from the germ of an idea to what you hold in your hand, and I want to thank them all most sincerely:

- The United Church of Canada Foundation and Grants Officer Eric Lo Forte for believing that this was worth investigating

- Peter MacIntosh and the superb folks at Narrative Research (Halifax) for their patient support of our emerging questionnaire and the multiple COVID-related delays
- The Board of Governors of Pine Hill Divinity Hall and Brenda Munro, Executive Director, for their support
- The Library staff at the Atlantic School of Theology who managed to find gold from my obscure requests for help
- Debbie Anderson, Carly Cumpstone, and the staff at Friesen Press who made it possible to put this text in your hands
- From the General Council of the United Church of Canada: Adam Hanley (Program Coordinator for Ministry Personnel Vitality), Deb Kigar (ChurchHub Specialist – Data Support and Training), and Susan Jackson (Information & Statistics Coordinator) all came through with crucial support when it was most needed
- My colleagues in the Association of United Church Clergy who take clergy well-being with utmost seriousness
- Erin Labrie who edited the text for spelling and grammar and clarity
- Jane Bolivar, Continuing Education Convenor, AST, who facilitated the initial workshop exploration of our findings
- Our many survey respondents and those who agreed to be interviewed
- The following read and commented on portions or all of the text and I thank them for their interest and support: Rob Fennell, Heather Hemming, David Hewitt, Phil Kennedy, Susan MacAlpine-Gillis, and Linda Yates
- My colleague in research and in ministry, the Rev. Kate Jones
- My spouse Heather, who listened to and encouraged me through the many twists and turns of this project.

+ + +

Rev. Kate Jones is an ordained minister in the United Church of Canada, currently serving Two Rivers Pastoral Charge in southern New Brunswick. Prior to her ordination in 2018, she had an 18-year career as a physiotherapist, including several years of being bi-vocational while completing her theological studies. Her current call is full-time so doesn't allow her the time to work in physiotherapy, however her identity is still bi-vocational as both a minister and a physiotherapist.

Rev. Dr. I. Ross Bartlett is the United Church Formation Director at the Atlantic School of Theology. Prior to that he had a thirty-eight-year career in congregational ministry, including part-time and full time bi-vocational appointments and calls. He has been involved in education and training for lay leaders and clergy for over twenty-five years. He has been the preaching columnist for *Gathering* magazine for fifteen years. Recent books include *Gathered for Preaching* (UCRD) and *On Holy Ground: You and Your Faith Story*. He also consults with clergy and congregations.

INTERVIEW PARTICIPANTS

As a final step in the survey process, respondents were invited to indicate if they were willing to be contacted for a longer in-depth interview. An astonishing 87% volunteered! From that group we chose several people who represented various trends in the data in order to develop a more in-depth and personal understanding of the different factors. All personal data has been anonymized.

George *is a middle-aged ordained minister whose family has had several clergy over the generations. He currently serves a mid-sized congregation on a half-time call, while working as the executive director of a not-for-profit housing agency. Previously he drew pay from both, a continual source of stress as the NFP was dependent on grants for funding and he was the writer of the applications. His situation changed several years ago when the congregation received a sizeable bequest and altered the terms of his call to employ him full-time while building in half-time work at the NFP. He is happy with his circumstances as he has long felt the call to social justice ministry but also struggled to support himself and his family in that work. For him it is important that part-time ministry does not equal every Sunday. He leads worship two of four weeks, attends on one of the others and is elsewhere for the fourth Sunday of the month. He also does funerals and emergency pastoral care and a "minimal amount" of administration. He is constantly watching out for lay people to "mentor" into leadership roles in various ministries. George acknowledges difficulty with boundaries and so builds in time away. He's brushed burn-out a couple of times in his career and lists having a spiritual guide and very strong practices as safeguards.*

Robert *entered training for diaconal ministry after retiring from the civil service. His government pension allows him to work for part-time pay (75% time) and he consciously "Chose to leave full time to younger new grads." He is still serving the same charge where he began his ministry almost a decade ago. As an older person, he feels he connects well with the community which is primarily composed of retirees. Along with worship and pastoral care ("keeping in touch") he has a particular passion for fostering an ecumenical cluster that focuses on a particular social justice issue. Having followed two or three part-time clergy, he found the congregation well-adapted to that style of ministry and feels they have "moved to post-survival mode" and are thriving in this new place. He finds that being physically active and making sure he gets plenty of rest are crucial to maintaining balance in his life. Balancing responsibilities and saying "no" are often times when he feels very conflicted and pressured, and he wishes he had more support, both from congregational and judicatory leadership, in maintaining boundaries. He also noted that the absence of administrative support is a huge burden limiting his effectiveness.*

Claire *is a long-serving diaconal minister who considers herself to be bi-vocational but hangs onto the part-time label as a means of responding to inappropriate expectations. "When I say to the church, 'sorry, you don't have enough of me,' it's a way of communicating the structural limitations and protecting herself. She always anticipated working full-time. Her primary interests were in education and youth ministry, and, for a number of years, she was able to focus there. By the early 1990s, the number of appropriate positions had declined significantly and she found herself doing solo ministry in a rural pastoral charge. After leaving ministry for more than a decade to pursue a position in government service, she returned to congregational ministry a few years ago. Her congregation is the one that she attended while working in government and, as the number of preaching points dwindled and finding a minister became harder, she gradually moved into wider leadership roles, initially on a supply basis and then under part-time appointment. So, she has significant roots in the pastoral charge and has shared important recent history. She made the conscious decision that, at her place in life, she could manage with 50% income, and she wanted time to pursue other activities. Claire has had a very mixed experience with the structures of the church, which she names as the discomfort those in the system had when she "didn't fit the normal slots they had." She also experienced suspicion and doubt from full-time colleagues concerning her level of commitment. She is convinced that interest and employment outside the church makes her "a better minister." The fact that the congregation is really interested in only Sunday is both a blessing and a frustration for her.*

Roberta is in her tenth year of ordained ministry in her current, single-point charge. It had been part of a two-point charge, but there was a bad split and now "they'd rather shut the doors than work with anyone else." She has always been in part-time ministry, having been settled into one. She feels that when she began, she and her peers were told that this was the only way into ministry and, "after a while" there would be full-time work. That has never happened for her. After skirting bankruptcy and contemplating leaving ministry, she finally secured employment spread between two geographically separate charges. After another difficult few years, she arrived in her current setting, "a part-time ministry that is really a part-time ministry so I know that I'm lucky." Part-time ministry allows her flexibility to travel and to be present to her family. The congregation is very supportive of her and recognizes that her elderly parents (she is an only child) are in another province. She identified the assumptions of people outside the church as a major challenge as well as the diminished opportunities to build collegial relationships. She is definitely not part-time by choice and feels it is a major failing of the church to allow the growth of part-time vacancies. She despairs of "making it to 65," because there is so much to do and so little support.

Juanita is an ordained minister serving her second part-time appointment since ordination. She has a passion for faith-based social justice work and is currently employed 75% time. While always entertaining the possibility of full-time work, she also realized that her diversity of interests and skills might lead to other paths. She is grateful to have connected with a not for profit that can pay her for her non-church work which she clearly sees as ministry. As a three-quarter-time employee, she conducts worship on three Sundays and uses the fourth as she chooses. She appreciates the flexibility of the congregation in honouring the part-time nature of her position. She calls it "a high trust environment" where she feels comfortable reminding people of the limitations. Because of the relationship they have developed, congregants accept that declaration of limits with no suspicions of her commitment or motivation. Finances are a challenge at 75% time and, as housing costs increase across the country, that creates additional stress. A further tension arises when she is expected to give leadership in other congregations/Regional activities without financial compensation. If she says yes to those opportunities, it impacts her ability to take on paid work or comes out of the congregation's time. At the same time, being able to identify herself as "Rev. Juanita" is sometimes helpful in establishing credibility in other work she takes on.

Catherine initially intended to become a psychologist or social worker before receiving a very strong call to ministry. Now, after subsequent training, she combines ministry with counselling and music. Her ministry appointment is for twenty-five hours a week. She serves a small, multi-cultural congregation that is combined with a much older, primarily white group. The move to part-time comes after a career of full-time and then part-time calls. Along the way she has had experience with burnout and ministry-related trauma. Working part-time allows her time for her spouse and her grandchildren, as well as her music.

Barbara is a candidate, serving part-time in a Supervised Ministry Placement. She has completed her MDiv in an on-campus program. She also works for a NFP in an educational role. While she can see full-time work as a possible future, she had a model of a part-time bi-vocational ministry in the church growing up. During her candidacy pathway and education there were very few models and little conversation about the possibility. Another bi-vocational minister shared with Barbara the challenges she received from full-time colleagues which often sound like judgments. Her employment with the NFP provides her with a wider viewpoint and with technical expertise that was very useful during the pandemic.

Marlene entered the BTh program at the age of 40 and spent seven full-time years in her first charge. She retired in 2020 and currently serves as retired supply on a 50%-time appointment. In between pastoral appointments she served for several years in a Conference staff role and, in 2017, began a small business related to different modalities of spiritual practice. She also accepted different offers to do pulpit supply which led to an offer of appointment to the same charge she had served at the beginning of her ministry. She says, "It felt like going home." A major challenge has been how to accommodate her pastoral work and her business, both of which she clearly experiences as ministry. The current model is two weeks of full-time, followed by two weeks entirely off. So far, that is going very well. She celebrates the willingness of the congregation to work with her to discover an appropriate rhythm. She also acknowledges the challenges of "staying away" during the two weeks where she is not doing pastoral charge work. Because of her previous roles the wider church was supportive, and the congregation had experienced part-time ministry before — easing many challenges. She feels she has found her stride in establishing her priorities and can think of only one instance where there was a conflict — "and we worked that out". Careful scheduling, honouring days off, and maintaining her own spiritual disciplines are key to her well-being. For the congregation, they are exposed to new ideas from guest worship leaders and understand the breadth of ministries that go on. She has several suggestions for better equipping new ministers for part-time realities.

Andrea was involved in social justice work with a variety of NFPs and government agencies before entering ministry. Most of her classmates were also second career people with family obligations, so *she felt very much at home. She followed a community-based program over a few years before her commissioning in 1989. She is currently serving a 50%-time retired supply appointment with a United Church congregation that is moving towards a shared ministry with another denomination in her small town. One interesting feature of the relationship is that, while Andrea ministered in a few other congregations, her family lived in the town where she now serves and attended the congregation over nearly four decades. So, she was very familiar with the context and the people. More than a decade ago the congregation faced a huge financial deficit and, with Presbytery support, were able to fund a transitional ministry which explored what it meant to be the people of God in that place, including the relationship to the building and to money. They left their building behind and consciously shifted from "a culture of poverty" which did not correspond to the actual socio-economic status of the members. The end of the transition resulted in a change to the terms of her call and she added another, part-time, shared ministry in order to make full-time work. That was a valuable experience when she retired and took up her current part-time appointment. The two denominations are joined in an important way by their openness to the LGBTQ+ community (which is not the norm for churches in their part of the country).*

When Andrea was commissioned, she could already see "that the idea of one minister for one congregation was already disappearing before our eyes." However, that was still the official picture – I knew that was not what I was doing. The diaconal skills that I acquired at College were whatever I needed to support the rural congregation." She worked full time in solo calls/appointments for a decade before moving to part-time and working in different sites to create full-time employment. She has many observations about the way in which the church views part-time ministry: "Too often part-time ministry is seen as you simply take the full-time job description and cut it in half. You simply can't do that. Convincing people that there has to be a different way to do that." She also feels that monetary issues, while important, are too often allowed to drive the decision.

She is also critical of the way in which the wider church views and supports its part-time clergy. She feels that the system is so oriented to full-time that it excludes the wider participation of part-time ministers. Her participation is only possible because she is retired: it's "a hobby."

QUESTIONS FOR REFLECTION

1. Do you know anyone who is part-time in ministry or any congregations that have ministers employed part-time? Have you talked to them about what that is like for them, the joys and challenges?

2. Have you ever worked two jobs at once? Was it by choice or by necessity? What was that like? What would you say (or imagine) are the special benefits and challenges of two (or more) jobs?

3. What is/are the most important activities for a congregational minister to do? Where are the places that lay people could step up? What would need to change for that to work?

ENDNOTES

[1] The Indigenous ministries of the United Church of Canada have both resources and questions beyond the scope of this book. Thus, this study deal only with the non-Indigenous regions.

Introduction

Seen from the outside, it may be hard to tell one church from another. Those with inside knowledge can sometimes tell the building of one tradition from others. In some places, it looks like all of the churches in one denomination got together for a paint sale because they're the same colour. Congregations take great pride in the upkeep of their buildings so the condition of the structure may not give you many hints either. But those on the inside know how quickly change is sweeping through these churches that were once bastions of their community. Many of them are spending more than they take in. Sometimes it's on building maintenance but more often it's staff salaries primarily the minister or pastor.

Clearly, it's not because those clergy are overpaid. Most pastors in mainline Canadian churches (Anglican, Presbyterian, Lutheran, United Church) are not in it for the money. And that's a good thing. Those denominations have salary and benefit charts which provide an element of justice in employment practices. But salary (which may or may not include housing), benefits, and so on, struggle to keep up to expenses. This is particularly so for relatively new clergy. For instance, in 2022, someone who has been credentialed in the United Church for two years earns the munificent sum of between $37,500 and $38,700 if they live in a church-owned home and roughly $49,000 if they are providing their own housing. This after six to ten years of university. Of course, those aren't the only amounts the congregation is responsible for, so by the time various benefits, government requirements, and expenses are included congregations are facing significant expenses. In almost every congregation I served in more than three decades, I was the largest single item in the church budget.

Often in those circumstances congregations feel that their only choice is to enter a part-time situation. That is a phenomenon that is sweeping across the mainline congregations. In my day job, I'm privileged to share the training and education of candidates for United Church ministry. A couple of years ago I recognized that, even though a growing number of my students would spend some or all of their careers in part-time ministry, as an instructor I knew very little about those realities. My own years of part-time ministry are a long way back in the rear-view mirror of my life. I was shocked to discover that my denomination knew very little about this development too. So, I went looking for some information to help my students and discovered a movement which may offer a new, healthy, and sustainable vision of church, my church and perhaps yours too. I discovered part-time and bi-vocational clergy who, simply by their existence, challenge some of our core views of the church and open the possibility of unleashing a significant new wave of Christian mission.

What's Coming?

Chapter 1 explores the history and theology of part-time and bi-vocational ministry. We begin there because there is an almost 1,800-year history of part-time clergy. Put it another way: the model of a full-time religious professional serving a single congregation is an historical oddity. The twentieth century mainline church (for all its many failings) often did wonderful ministry for God and neighbour. That model worked for a period of time. However, since many of those leading today's mainline congregations (clergy and lay) came out of that form of church, it's hard to imagine another way, a way that has significant potential for our present and future.

Chapter 2 reports the results of the largest survey of part-time clergy undertaken in a mainline Canadian denomination. A survey completed by 240 part-time United Church currently serving in positions addresses who they are, how they spend their time, their joys and struggles, what they wished the church knew. From the survey respondents we conducted nine in-depth interviews with individuals who seemed to embody some of the dominant characteristics.

In chapter 3 we look at the ways in which mainline denominations have been responding to shrinking numbers (members and money) for thirty years and we discover that this is not a new phenomenon at all. It has simply reached the magnitude that we must take is seriously.

The main location for part-time ministry is the congregation, so in chapter 4 we look at what part-time ministry often means for the local community of faith and what it could mean if we thought about it differently.

In chapter 5 we will look in more detail at some different models of congregational life that offer the hope for a sustainable, viable, and exciting future.

In chapter 6 we turn our attention to the next generation of clergy and start to answer some of the questions that started me on this quest: what can we do differently and better to help these wonderful people thrive in this new environment?

Church Structures: Who does What?

Mainline denominations are human, and they have their own labels for who does what. This study is grounded in the United Church of Canada, but it has broad applicability across mainline denominations in Canada and the United States and beyond. To help you translate what is said here, it may help to identify the players (more detail is found in the appendix)

The national governing and policy setting body is the General Council. There is an executive that conducts the denomination's work between the every-three-year Council meetings. Also at the national level is the Office of Vocation, responsible for the oversight and discipline of clergy and setting standards for candidates to meet. The church is divided into sixteen geographic Regions of roughly similar numbers of members. There is also an Indigenous Region which is not geographic, however the gifts and challenges of the Indigenous Church fall outside this study. The Regions are responsible for the pastoral relations process, the various steps by which clergy and congregations are connected. The local expression of the church is the Congregation or Community of Faith (the terms are interchangeable). This may be a single congregation, or two or more congregations linked by a common governance structure (a multi-point pastoral charge).

The United Church has three streams of paid, accountable ministry, each with different ethos and training programs.[1] Diaconal Ministers are *commissioned* to the ministry of "Education, Service and Pastoral Care" generally after completing a four-year diploma in Diaconal Ministry Studies. This is an in-community program where students are working (often in ministries) and studying simultaneously. Designated Lay Ministers are *recognized* following a three-year program of study which involves in-community ministry. Ordained ministers, *ordained* to the ministry of "Word, Sacrament and Pastoral Care", complete a Master of Divinity (MDiv) degree, either as a three-year on-campus program or as five-year in ministry stream. While the different education/training institutions exercise great freedom in terms of the content and delivery mechanisms of their programs, the United Church, through the Office of Vocation establishes some required core subjects.

Diaconal Ministers
commissioned
"Education, Service & Pastoral Care"
Designated Lay Ministers
recognized
Ordained Ministers
ordained
"Word, Sacrament and Pastoral Care"

The Challenge of Change

Speaking of ministry and congregations in an inquiring fashion is often risky. It is easy for readers to think that what is dear to them is being criticized or mocked. So, from the outset I want to declare the deep and abiding respect we have for the clergy and the congregations who are serving God, neighbour, and creation in so many faithful ways. Many of them are living in inherited ways that have borne rich fruit over the decades. One of the aspects of contemporary church life that I would love to see banished is a sense of "failing." If we are not as successful (pick

Regardless of the number of hours in the call or appointment, clergy consider themselves to be fully the minister of the community of faith.

In this study, part-time is strictly a reference to the number of hours remunerated per week according to the call or appointment form.

your form of measurement) as that congregation (choose your favourite example of success), congregations sometimes lapse into feelings of guilt or despair. If the form or expression of ministry that has nurtured the community for generations no longer has wide appeal, we become convinced that it's our fault. If people do not rise up after Sunday morning worship to storm the barricades of injustice and bring about the city eternal on earth, we must be doing something wrong. The immodest goal here is to banish such language and thinking as unhealthy, unhelpful, and ultimately untrue. There is so much faithful life and work going on and (perhaps in typically Canadian modesty) we undervalue and under-celebrate it.

We will be advocating that some changes in our life together be considered. These arise from the research data and are presented for discussion and not as solutions. Some congregations will choose, for whatever reasons, not to embrace these suggestions. Some clergy will want to continue in ways of serving that have been rewarding and satisfying. That is not failure. As a church we have imbibed deeply our culture's images of success; many have no grounding in God's good news. There, amongst other things, we learn that everything has a season, including communities of faith. If a congregation can courageously face the truth that their time of service is drawing to a close, think of the wonderful ways service can be celebrated, legacies can be planned, grief can be honoured, and joy grasped. Our Puritan ancestors spoke of the good death, not as a reflection of the *how* of dying, but in the legacy that we left. We have clergy who have great skills in accompanying communities into that. Can we do a better job of acknowledging what is occurring and linking skills with need? That is part of the hope of this study.

Decades ago, Canadian theologian Douglas John Hall was alerting us to the end of Christendom: that period from the 300s on where the church has been at the centre of all parts of culture and society. He wrote of the many ways in which that centrality was being challenged and expressed. The growth of part-time and bi-vocational ministry may be another expression of that decentering of the mainline church. With such changes we must always ask, "where is God in this and how can we most faithfully be Christ's people." Our hope is that this study give some suggestions of possible directions.

QUESTIONS FOR DISCUSSION

1. Canadian theologian Douglas John Hall wrote about "the end of Christendom", moving the church from the centre of society. What evidence of that change do you see in your community? What impact do you think it has had on the quality of life and diversity?

2. If you are not United Church of Canada by tradition, can you name the individuals/ committees that do the tasks identified in this chapter?

3. If you are a church member, what do you know about your minister's/pastor's training? Are they first-career clergy or did they have previous employment? Have you ever asked them what they wish they might have learned before starting ministry?

ENDNOTES

[1] What follows are the typical education/training paths for the non-Indigenous church. There are many individual variations.

Looking at Our Story
With New Eyes

A complete history and theology of bi-vocational and part-time ministry is beyond the scope of this book. However, it is important to summarize the key points to establish the legitimacy of this vocational form, especially in the face of a full time, uni-vocational bias in the church.

Perhaps the best known bi-vocational Christian leader is the Apostle Paul who, according to the book of Acts, was a tentmaker by trade: "I worked with my own hands to support myself and my companions. . . In all this I gave you and example." (Acts 18:3; 20:34-35a). He apparently felt some ambivalence about this, telling others that "those who proclaim the gospel should get their living by the gospel," but also celebrating the fact that by his other work he was able to "make the gospel free of charge." (1 Cor 9:14-15a, 18). The mere fact that Paul models this life should not be seen as prescriptive, but it does establish a legitimate lineage. In other places, Paul relates his employment to the restricted finances of the congregation: "You remember our labour and toil, brothers and sisters; we worked night and day, so that we might not burden any of you while we proclaimed to you the gospel of God." (1 Thessalonians 2:9). This seems to have been less of a bedrock conviction than a tool for the furthering of the gospel, employed where it was appropriate and set aside in other circumstances.

It is difficult to determine when the model of a pastoral leader supported entirely by the congregation emerged. Early in the Christian story, we have accounts of those who withdrew to the desert and were supported by the gifts of others, but those holy hermits are not a model for ministry. Early Christian texts talk about hosting visiting preachers and prophets, but we cannot assume from that a model of total absorption in the spiritual feeding of others.[1]

In the third century we find Cyprian of Carthage overseeing a significant number of congregations in what is now North Africa. The prosperity of that centre of the Roman Empire led to the brief appearance of a model that would not reappear for a millennium and a half, full-time congregational leaders. With Cyprian, we hear the first arguments that clergy should be freed from the various mundane tasks of life (such as earning a living) to focus on more holy pursuits and congregational care. Because of the cost involved, it is unclear how widespread the practice became.[2]

After that brief flicker, the overwhelmingly predominant model was that clergy had other jobs as a necessity. You could not sustain life as a priest. The role might come with prestige and, at least according to the Protestant Reformers, way too many opportunities to make money on the side, but you were expected to follow a trade or to farm. Their education might lead to employment as clerks, lawyers, judges, or teachers. There was no concept of a progress through university education and graduate training for the purpose of making a living serving a congregation.

During the Protestant Reformation, great emphasis was placed on the minister as preacher. This was in response to various church practices which the reformers felt had silenced the bible as God's Word. Taking that to a logical conclusion, every Christian is also a preacher. Different reformers employed different phrasing. The most memorable may be Martin Luther's "the priesthood of all believers." Regardless of the phrasing, the result was a collapsing of the existing boundaries between laity and clergy and the dismissing of the higher spiritual status awarded to those who had given themselves most fully to religious service, nuns and monks. That dismissal of the category of full-time religious person also extended to clergy. In the popular medieval hierarchy, priests were seen as just slightly lower than monastics. If every Christian was a priest, then there was no place for full-time religious experts. According to Luther:

> God has placed his Church in the midst of the world amongst countless
> under-takings and callings in order that Christians should not be monks but
> live with one another in social fellowship and manifest among men the works
> and practices of faith.

The new idea was that all were priests but those called priests are ministers, admitted to certain functions on behalf of the congregation and in service to God. Moving this idea from theology to daily practice was challenging to say the least. Although Luther believed that the congregation was superior to the minister and could both call and remove them (solely for failure in fidelity to the Word of God) in actual life congregations were in no position to exercise that authority. The status afforded to preachers was such that they were largely unassailable.

John Calvin gave preachers equally high status because they were mouthpieces for God, not due to any personal piety or virtue. Other reformers took a similar position. In the confusion and various forms of institutional collapse as well as the different forms of governance that accompanied the Reformation, it is often difficult to determine the economic and employment status of clergy. Most jurisdictions appear to have had individuals in full-time roles as ecclesiastical authorities, overseeing congregations and ministers. For the congregational clergy it is less definite. Part of the challenge lies in the fact that we tend to differentiate aspects of our lives in a way that was unknown to them. As well, most of the records concern city churches where different economics applied than in villages. For a long time, clergy who wished to move from rural to town parishes had to be examined for theological and professional fitness because they were generally of lower educational standards. We know that most ministers came from the middle class: sons of teacher, clerks, typesetters, weavers, and so on. There were very few of the noble or peasant class. There were frequent complaints about their excessive drinking and their uncouth manners and clothing.

These behaviours were often linked by contemporaries to the poor economic conditions in which clergy lived. In the turmoil of the Reformation many of the former means of supporting the church ceased, and lands that had been parish church property were seized by local nobility. As a result, the revenue available was insufficient for ministers to live on. In 1531 Luther commented on the poverty of clergy and how frequently they turned to other means to eke out a living. Later, some standardization of pay was introduced, and town clergy might be paid as much as an outdoor labourer would earn in a year but less than a master builder meaning that they would need to supplement their income in some way simply to survive.

Cyprian's ideal was largely aspirational for most in the Christian world until the mid-nineteenth century. Certainly, there were some wealthy and important congregations in larger cities that could afford to have a full-time clergy, but they represented only a small fraction of the whole and constituted a mark of some prestige. In some places in England and Europe, there were special endowments that supported full-time scholars and preachers. In Canada, the "clergy reserves" in Upper Canada were made up of land set aside for the "support of Protestant clergy" (interpreted as Church of England only) in the Constitution Act (1791). The idea was that the leases paid by farmers for use of the land would go to maintain clergy. Because so much land was available for free, the reserves were largely unprofitable until 1819. After that, higher rates were charged, but it is not clear whether the revenues were sufficient to support any significant number of uni-vocational clerics.

In the predecessor denominations of the United Church of Canada, the Congregationalists and Presbyterians were the strongest promoters of the concept of the congregation fully supporting the minister. The Methodists, by contrast, were characterized in the early decades by the circuit rider; the preacher being hosted by several congregations at a rate of once a month or even less frequently. Given a constant shortage of clergy, it was common for lay people to undertake, as a natural expression of their discipleship, many ministries of pastoral care, education, social justice, and worship. Full-time clergy became more common as the nineteenth century moved into the twentieth and overall prosperity and disposable income increased. Starting from the wealthier cities the image of full-time clergy became the norm and an aspirational goal for congregations. The next step was for the full-time minister to gradually assume many of the tasks of the congregation, becoming a sort of expert Christian who made the efforts of others appear amateurish and second-rate. As many aspects of life became increasingly specialized it seemed to be a mark of progress to leave those activities to trained and skilled professionals. The result is that a majority of those in many communities of faith feel legitimately inadequate to take up those tasks that may previously have been addressed by full-time clergy.

This history and learned experience demonstrate that reclaiming the older tradition of part-time ministry will entail more than simply redrafting position descriptions and issuing new calls and appointments. There are deeply rooted norms to be addressed and the context of life and ministry has changed dramatically since part-time ministry was the expected pattern in Canadian Protestantism. The simple statement that, "We can't afford any more than this," uttered at a congregational meeting will not be sufficient. Both congregations and clergy will need assistance to understand and live into their new reality.

For instance, although they may not have personally experienced a strong heritage of lay ministry, many congregation members have significant skills and life experience that, with appropriate mentoring, can be turned to the congregation's ministry. Accessing this rich resource requires several changes. As well as willing participants, this rich future needs clergy who are sufficiently self-confident to accept vital lay ministry and have the skills to equip congregants to re-encounter the biblical and historical visions of discipleship and ministry. How often have we read Paul's list of the gifts given by the Spirit?

> *7To each is given the manifestation of the Spirit for the common good.8To one is given through the Spirit the utterance of wisdom, and to another the utterance of knowledge according to the same Spirit, 9to another faith by the same Spirit, to another gifts of healing by the one Spirit, 10to another the working of miracles, to another prophecy, to another the discernment of spirits, to another various kinds of tongues, to another the interpretation of tongues. 11All these are activated by one and the same Spirit, who allots to each one individually just as the Spirit chooses. 1 Corinthians 12:7-11*

In many cases, however, this is mostly aspirational in nature, desperately trying to convince individuals to take up their role in the congregation as we try and fill the various places in an organizational chart! Paul had his eye on something so much richer and more vibrant that is fully equipped to face whatever lies ahead in the particular role this congregation has in fulfilling God's mission in the world.

The concept of bi-vocational ministry is more than simply something that has *worked* over the centuries and conveniently addresses contemporary needs. To address concerns that it somehow falls short of the "true" model of ministry, namely a uni-vocational expression, it is helpful to explore how bi-vocational ministry can be seen as a possible representation of a core Christian doctrine. When we consider the multiplicity of the Divine as captured in the doctrine of the Trinity, we have another way of understanding this approach to ministry. Although we, as humans, are made in the Divine image, yet the One in whose image we are made is Three. However, the Three persons of God are named, the orthodox response is the same. Three persons, equal in Divinity, distinct from one another and yet inseparable in action and being.[3] The term assigned to that intra-trinitarian relationship is *perichoresis*. This is classically defined as "being-in-one-another, permeation without confusion."[4] The origins of the word in "dance around" or "round dance" heightens the appreciation of the inter-relatedness and interdependence of the Trinity's persons.

As we explored the identity of those expressing a call to bi-vocational ministry, we saw that weaving together repeated. There were distinct vocational identities that needed to operate together. The different identities were experienced as inseparable in operation and interacted in a *perichoretic* fashion. The challenges identified often related to moments when, for any number of reasons, the different vocational identities collided. Respondents referred to the apparent difficulty some people had reconciling their bi-vocational status with some ideal of a *real* or *genuine* minister. Some experienced a diminishment in the eyes of others, as if being bi-vocational meant they were somehow less faithful or less accomplished than their peers ("if you were a good minister, you'd be working full time"). Frustration was expressed over the lack of consideration given to their scheduling challenges when meetings were set, or pastoral care was expected.

Bi-vocational clergy develop a range of techniques and responses. Several saw the wearing of a clerical collar as a useful means of clarifying and distinguishing roles. There was a sense that the identification was as much for the minister herself as for the world around. When people saw them with the little tab at the neck, they were not likely to confuse them with the other identity. Such a strategy may be especially useful in situations where clergy might often be seen in either role (e.g., in a small community). Some respondents spoke of how extra effort was needed to maintain their pastoral identity, particularly in the wider church. They felt it was easy to be forgotten as part of the order of ministry. This seems particularly acute when there is a strong distinction between the identities and the role of minister would not be welcome or acceptable in the other setting. Instead of receiving help to work out logistical challenges of balancing multiple roles, one reports receiving suggestions (even from those close to them) that they give up ministry or go on the Discontinued Service List (Voluntary) for a time.[5] Contemplating the surrendering of the title of "Reverend" brought into sharp focus how central her pastoral identity was to her complete self-perception.

Respondents employed different means of expressing the relationship between their vocational expressions. The *perichorean* nature of existence inevitably creates tensions, both internal and external, which would be absent in a more singularly focused life. For some, the lack of extreme tension between their identities is a pleasant surprise. When they first surrendered to their bi-vocational calling and took up the other role, they had anticipated more difficulties than have emerged. While there is joyous relief in fully embracing the wholeness of identity, there can be issues of congruence. For example, some report struggling with the non-ministry workplace culture which is less open and compassionate or with the ministry setting, where the clearer objectives of a business must be weighed in association with other motivations and values.

Healthy self-differentiation and clear boundaries, important in full-time ministry, are crucial in bi-vocational and part-time calls/appointments. While a healthy life is not made up of a series of discrete boxes, respondents spoke of the need for clarity about different roles, close relationships, and self-care to make sure those vital aspects of life do not suffer. They cannot be entirely compartmentalized, however and respondents used dynamic terms like "juggle," "balance," "tension," "muddied," and "flow" as they spoke of

> *"It gets me out of the church bubble" George*

navigating their own unique *perichoresis.* The relationship is not always one of conflict. Each vocation may contribute to a more fully rounded understanding of the other, to the enhancement of both.

Thus, we find that both core doctrine and church history support a healthy respect for bi-vocational ministry, especially in situations where the ministry personnel can develop a sense of congruency in life and recognize that the various roles and identities are not static but fluid in their constant influencing of one another.

QUESTIONS FOR DISCUSSION

1. What part of this history of ministry was new information for you? What new insights have you had? How can you explore those further?

2. When you think about ministers in congregations, do you imagine them to be full-time? Have you ever known a part-time or bi-vocational minister?

3. George says that being bi-vocational gets him "out of the church bubble." Why do you think he enjoys that? What benefits can you imagine that being bi-vocational provides ministers? What benefits for the congregation? What might be some challenges to overcome if the minister is part-time?

ENDNOTES

[1] We acknowledge that there are Deuteronomic references to supporting priests which fall outside the scope of this paper. More relevant instances might be Lydia and Dorcas although the degree to which their important work supported their own direct ministry is unclear.

[2] H.R. Niebuhr and D.D. Williams, *The Ministry in Historical Perspectives*, (New York: Harper and Brothers, 1956), 8.

[3] Kathryn Tanner, *Christ the Key* (Cambridge: Cambridge University Press, 2010), 148.

[4] Kate Jones, "Who Am I? Bi-vocational Ministers and Pastoral Identity", (unpublished paper, Atlantic School of Theology, 2017), pg 11, quoting Catherine Mowry LaCugna, *God For Us: The Trinity and Christian Life* (New York: HarperCollins Publishers, 1991), 271.

[5] The United Church maintains two lists of clergy whose status as functioning ministers has been suspended. Both are called Discontinued Service Lists, the difference being between Voluntary and Disciplinary. The former is an option for those who, for whatever reason, wish to suspend their ministerial function for a time. The latter is the United Church's version of de-frocking, removing from an individual the rights, privileges and responsibilities of their credentials.

What's the Big Picture?

We had four large questions when we started this study.

1. What are the work and personal situations of part-time clergy?
2. What are the key challenges they confront?
3. How are part-time clergy viewed by their congregations?
4. Is there a correlation between work habits and perceptions, on the one hand, and the challenges faced by ministers on the other hand? How might these insights inform future strategies around part-time ministry?

Our primary tool was an online survey with credentialled part-time clergy members of the United Church of Canada.[1] A total of 240 useable surveys were collected, each of which required an average of twenty-two minutes to complete. The survey ran from April 16 to June 23, 2021. Fair warning, the information from the survey was shocking in some ways! Depending on your assumptions about the church and ministry it may leave you shaken. However, to fully enter the new possibilities that lie ahead we need to comprehend what is actually happening at the moment and how we arrived here. We believe that the future, although very different from our recent past as mainline churches, is filled with possibility.

Setting the Stage

To understand the insights that developed it's probably helpful to have some context. Like most mainline denominations the United Church of Canada has been shrinking in recent decades. In fact, like many denominations, the

	2000	2015	2021
Preaching Points	3,709	2,894	2,649
Pastoral Charges	2,351	2,1825	2,008

last time membership grew was in the mid-1960s, but it took a while for awareness of that to dawn.

According to a General Council report in 2017[2] the number of preaching points (individual congregations) declined from 3,709 in 2000 to 2,894 in 2015 and the number of pastoral charges from 2,351 to 2,128.[3] As of September 2017, the 650 part-time roles were being filled as follows: 134 part-time appointments were served by retired supply ministers; 91 part-time appointments and 238 part-time calls were being served by ordained and diaconal clergy (pre-retirement); and, 113 part-time appointments were being served by designated lay ministers. If we consider trends, they look somewhat like this:

135 PT retired supply

91 PT appointments

238 PT Calls

113 PT DLM

Year	Total Clergy	Full-time	Part-time
2008	2,250	1,650	600 (26.6% of total)
2012	2,125	1,500	625
2016	1,900	1,250	650
2021	1,602	972	628 (39.2% of total)

Number of Hours listed on Call/Appointment Form

15% 16 hours or less

51% 17-20 hours

33% 21+ hours

The date of that forecast is significant because it is the last time that a projection of the numbers of part-time clergy was made that is available to the public. The picture for 2030 was that a total of 1,474 clergy would be serving 1,918 pastoral charges. It was projected that part-time calls/appointments would go from 26.6% of the total in 2008 to 44.5% in 2030 and the number of denominational members would drop from 326 (2000) per serving minister to 185 by 2030. Those numbers are shocking but as we will see, the reality is even starker.

We learned a lot about the people who participated in our research: 43% are in called positions and 57% in appointments. In terms of length of time in ministry, they ranged from six years and less (22%), through seven to twenty years (37%), to more than twenty-one years (41%). They came from every part of Canada and Bermuda apart from Newfoundland and Labrador.[4] Thirty percent were 25-55 years old; 68% were more than 55 years; 2 % declined to answer. The number of hours of work per week specified in the employment documents ranged from 16 hours or less (15%), through 17-20 hours (51%) to 21 hours and more (33%). They were predominately ordained (70%), follow by DLM (12%), diaconal (9%), and candidate (8%).[5]

Most of these folk (83%) are the only clergy in their setting.[6] Most serve a single congregation (67%) or two congregations (25%) with only a handful (7%) responsible for three or more. In an interesting detail, you are slightly more likely to be ordained if you have one congregation and slightly more likely to be DLM (followed

Number of Years Served in Ministry

22% 6 years or less

37% 7-20 years

41% 21 years or more

by diaconal and candidate) if you have two or more. It is consistent with that for the majority (75%) to conduct only one service per week, with the remainder conducting two or more. The later in life you were credentialled the more likely it is that you will be conducting more than one service per week.

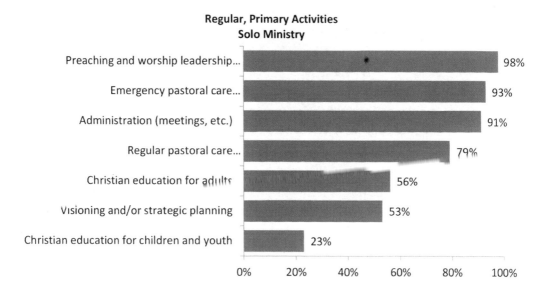

Regular, Primary Activities
Solo Ministry

Activity	Percentage
Preaching and worship leadership...	98%
Emergency pastoral care...	93%
Administration (meetings, etc.)	91%
Regular pastoral care...	79%
Christian education for adults	56%
Visioning and/or strategic planning	53%
Christian education for children and youth	23%

Those serving in part-time calls/appointments were remarkably consistent in identifying their primary tasks in each week as: worship and preaching (98%), emergency pastoral care (93%), and administration (91%) with more regular pastoral care a distant fourth (79%). We will have reason to return to these figures but at this point we merely wish to note with concern that Christian education for adults (56%) and strategic planning (53%) rank comparatively low as priorities which raises concerns for the future and ministry of these Communities of Faith. Our suspicion is that, in the way in which part-time ministry is currently conceived, there is simply neither time

"The observation of 'there's not enough time to do everything' to me it begs the question of who is or isn't helping get things done. Less a question of decision making, more a question of ministry support." - Workshop participant

nor energy for these activities that are more future-oriented. 91% of respondents report discussing their ministry priorities with the governing body of the congregation. That a healthy number of these clergy find themselves working beyond the number of hours stated in the call/appointment forms will come as no surprise. That would be consistent with the experience of many ministers. What is surprising is that 47% report that they generally have the time to accomplish the desired tasks. The 61% who feel they need to work more than the allotted hours on a regular or frequent basis, work an average of 6.4 extra (39%, 4-6 hours; 27%, 7-10 hours). The most frequently cited reason given for this behaviour is that there is "too much to do" in the allotted time. This ought to serve as a signal about the choices and priorities being made by clergy and their congregations. Somebody, somewhere in the system, has identified priorities which cannot be contained within the allotted hours. 40% of those working more than the agreed hours see it as an expression of discipleship; 28% acknowledge that they have difficulty saying "no"; and 21% say that they have a particular project or passion that leads to their overworking. These factors raise a level of concern as the denomination discusses the sustainability and faithfulness of part-time calls/appointments.

Along with the basic data of how many and how much, we also wanted to attempt a picture of satisfaction, employment issues, and places where changes might be made. Overall, eight in ten report that their congregations understand the constraints of part-time ministry. This understanding is less likely (54%) if the minister has no other employment and more likely (80%) if the position is sixteen hours a week or less. The evident conclusion is that other, non-ministry employment or highly abbreviated hours provide an important buffer for "ministry creep" and creates clearer boundaries for everyone in the covenant. Making choices is a constant in any ministry position, a reality magnified in part-time calls/appointments. 70% report having sought and received support in making their priority choices, with 75% accessing the Ministry and Personnel Committee and 57% the governing body.[7]

It is evident that newer ministers, those credentialled the fewest years, face more challenges in ministry. For instance, fewer years in ministry:

- Correlates with a negative response to the statement: "I have enough time to accomplish tasks"[8]
- Correlates with working more than the stipulated hours[9]
- Correlates with greater challenges in balancing responsibilities, addressing congregational expectations, and employment uncertainty
- Correlates with a negative response to the question of comfort with time use and priorities[10]
- Correlates with a greater desire for full-time employment[11]

Those with a shorter tenure are also somewhat less inclined to feel supported by the Regional Minister, the Region, and the Office of Vocation, as compared to those 21+ years.

Of course, some of these results could be a matter of finding one's way in a new role. But it also suggests some places where intervention by schools and regions might be helpful in increasing the sense of well-being and the longevity of early calls and appointments.

The polity of the United Church relies

"I honestly don't think that I can make it to 65 in this profession – I just don't think I can do it. I'm hoping I can make it to Freedom-55. The reason why is I find that there isn't a lot of support for what I do. Now that we've gone to the Regional structures, I have almost no communication with anybody any more." – Claire

heavily on the active participation of clergy and laity in a range of policy-setting and decision-making bodies. It also mandates that Communities of Faith without "regularly settled ministers" (called or appointed) must have an off-site supervisor. Similarly, all candidates under appointment require a trained supervisor. Most, although certainly not all, of these supervisors are clergy in their own pastoral ministries. As a result, the degree of involvement of part-time clergy in the wider life of the church is of great significance as their numbers rapidly increase. Our study reveals that only half of the part-time ministers (49%) are involved in the work of the wider church although 71% say that their congregations see this as a legitimate part of the covenant. Interestingly, if you serve in British Columbia or Alberta, the congregation is far more likely to support that work.

> *"[There is] No room in the part-time for participation in wider church. Involvement in wider church is a hobby. Only works because I have time." – Andrea*

The denomination will need to be attentive to the participation and support rates due to their potential impact on denominational functioning.

What about the non-ministry part of life? 32% of respondents said that they would prefer to be employed in ministry full-time. The longer one has been in ministry the less likely the interest in full-time employment (which correlates with what we will see around income sources). What are some of the factors impacting those wishing to be fulltime? Many are constrained by non-ministry factors such as family responsibilities (25%), an inability to relocate geographically (35%), and a shortage of full-time calls/appointments within a reasonable commuting distance (58%).

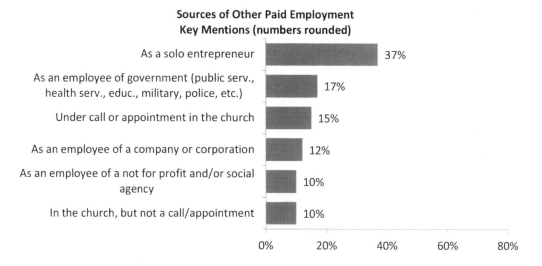

The sixty-eight per cent who firmly opted for part-time cited: the freedom to pursue other activities (45%); sufficient income due to pension or partner income (28%); call to non-ministry activities (16%), and the constraints of family responsibilities (11%). Ministerial salaries are not particularly large so how do they make ends meet? 49% are receiving pension income (of those 70% are United Church or other denomination pensioners), which also includes CPP and other employers (17%). 26% of those happy with part-time status have other paid employment:

37% as a solo entrepreneur

17% as some form of government employee

12% with a company

10% with a not for profit

10% in the church but not a call or appointment

68% of respondents consider their non-ministry work to be a vocation – as much an expression of their faith and discipleship as their ministry involvement.

The older you were at age of credentialling the less likely you are to have other employment or significant pension income. In addition to employment, 60% of part-time clergy are engaged in significant volunteer activity of more than ten hours a week, an amount that is likely to increase the larger the number of hours contracted to work.

Respondents were asked to identify their relationship to their non-ministerial work:

Of the full-time respondents, 5% identified as bi-vocational

Of the part-time respondents, 33% identified as bi-vocational

Of the part-time respondents, 51% said they merely had another job

Of the part-time respondents, 10% had no response

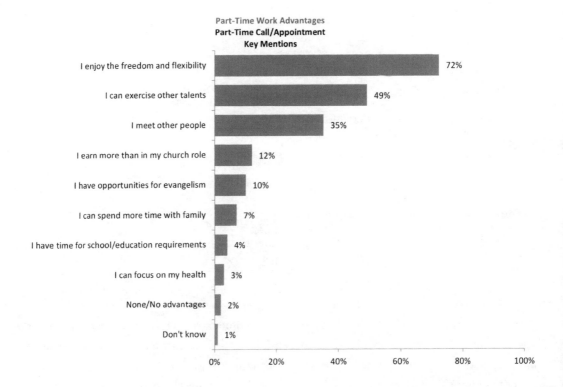

Part-Time Work Advantages
**Part-Time Call/Appointment
Key Mentions**

Advantage	Percentage
I enjoy the freedom and flexibility	72%
I can exercise other talents	49%
I meet other people	35%
I earn more than in my church role	12%
I have opportunities for evangelism	10%
I can spend more time with family	7%
I have time for school/education requirements	4%
I can focus on my health	3%
None/No advantages	2%
Don't know	1%

When asked what they would like the wider church to understand, respondents listed: the value of my work (19%); that I choose to be part-time (11%); that part-time *employment* is not the same as a part-time *vocation*; that there was more understanding/support for smaller churches (8%); that there was more support/resources for part-time clergy (7%); the breadth of skills that part-time ministers bring (6%). In terms of institutional support, 65% feel valued by Regional Minister (the staff person responsible for pastoral relations); 58% by the regional structure as a whole; and 54% by the Office of Vocation. This support is less felt by those who are younger (twenty-five to thirty-five years of age), in appointments rather than calls, and/or employed 16 hours a week or fewer. It is worth noting that, across the board, clergy in Alberta and British Columbia are more likely to report feeling valued and supported by wider church structures and staff.

> How do we educate our congregations about what part time ministry looks like?
> Workshop participant

In the rest of this study, we will unpack some of the meaning of those numbers.

QUESTIONS FOR DISCUSSION

1. What aspects of the survey results surprised you the most?
2. What new insights into the life of a part-time minister did you gain?
3. The survey uncovered a number of challenges for part-time ministers. How would address any of them?

ENDNOTES

[1] See Appendix 1 for methodology and survey.

[2] https://unitedchurch.sharepoint.com/sites/UnitedChurchCommons/PublicDocuments/Forms/AllItems.aspx?id=%2Fsites%2FUnitedChurchCommons%2FPublicDocuments%2FShared%2DPublicly%2FGovernance%2FPC%2DMEPS%2FDemographic%20Report%20Presentation%202017%2Epdf&parent=%2Fsites%2FUnitedChurchCommons%2FPublicDocuments%2FShared%2DPublicly%2FGovernance%2FPC%2DMEPS, accessed November 25, 2021.

[3] Prior to the change in governance structure in 2019, the basic unit of organization was the Pastoral Charge which might consist of one or a number of preaching points generally served by the same clergyperson.

[4] The United Church has a long-standing connection with the Methodist Church in Bermuda.

[5] Individuals preparing for credentialling are eligible for appointment as candidate supply, serving in pastoral ministry under direct supervision.

[6] The number of people reporting being part of a team is quite small, weakening the reliability of the data. The indicators are that most of the reports are for people in a pastoral care role and 68% of those teams include at least one fulltime minister.

[7] In the United Church all congregations are required to have a Ministry and Personnel Committee (regardless of name) to consult and support staff, oversee the staff-congregation relationship, review working conditions and responsibilities, addressing position descriptions amongst other things. *The Manual*, 2021, sect 8.7.8.5.

[8] 6yrs experience or less 7%; 7-20 years of experience 10%; 21+ years of experience 20%

[9] 6yrs of experience or less 66%; 7-20 years of experience 65%; 21+ years of experience 55%

[10] Overall, 90% are comfortable with these. Of those who are not: 6 years and less 41%; 7-20 years 33%; 21+ years 49%

[11] Those who wish they were in full-time ministry comprise 41% of those with 6yrs experience or less, 37% of those with 7-20 years, and 18% of those with 21+ years.

What do we Mean by Part-time?
More than you Might Imagine!

Even though I spent some time doing part-time ministry in my graduate school days, I was surprised by the scope of differences covered by a seemingly straightforward term. As we saw in the first chapter it is certainly not new in the Christian story. But it is an expression of ministry that is growing in Canada and has been for some time, whether or not we've been aware of it.

In a 2015 article, Sam Reimer and Rick Hiemstra studied Revenue Canada charitable forms (T0310) for a significant number of congregations over a ten-year period.[1] This was the first (and thus far only) large-scale study of its kind in Canada and revealed the virtually universal trend to part-time positions in both Roman Catholic and Protestant denominations. They provided depth to Reginald Bibby's observation at the beginning of the decade: declining participation was leading to shrinking budgets, partially reflected in ministerial staffing levels.[2] Reimer and Hiemstra went on to argue that budgets were not the sole reason for the change and to speculate about the impact on the quality of ministry. Unfortunately, from our perspective, their focus was largely on Roman Catholic and Evangelical churches where, as we will see, the policies and practices do not entirely map onto those of the United Church. However, given the dearth of study of this phenomenon in Canada, some interaction with their conclusions may be helpful to us.

To begin with, they note that "part-time" employment is a growing phenomenon in all sectors across the Western world. In Canada, in 1953, part-time work made up only 3% of the labour force while by 2009 it made up 26.9% for women and 11.6% for men (19.1% overall).[3] The experience of the COVID-19 pandemic and what some observers label the "great resignation" indicate that the wider trend continues as we have seen it within the church. Part-time is simply more common throughout all aspects of the Canadian labour force. They explore several factors of which three seem particularly relevant to our consideration: the tightening of budgets, employers seeking more flexibility in their workforce, and what the authors label,

1953 3% of Canadian labour force identified at part-time

2009 26.9% of women; 11.6% men identified as part-time (19.1% overall).

the "feminization of employment norms." This latter trend they explain as a reflection of historic conditions of women's work: lower pay, temporary, and part-time. They do allow for both the voluntary selection of part-time work and the possibility of working full-time *and* living in poverty.[4]

Focussing more particularly on churches they offer several concerns. There is a documented correlation between clergy well-being and congregational well-being[5]. To some observers, the growth of part-time work leads to "volunteer-led and therefore vulnerable congregations."[6] While our study indicates that the lack of professional leadership can certainly create instability in congregations, we will suggest that part-time ministry, where it is genuinely embraced as a positive factor, can result in a much higher level of lay involvement providing its own source of stability.

Leaving aside their study of Roman Catholic and Evangelical congregations, the Reimer/Heimstra study provides some historical context for our focus. Speaking of mainline congregations[7] that filed charitable returns in 2003 and 2011 they note the following staff changes. The table shows the number of congregations with full-time (FT) and part-time (PT) pastors in each group and the percentage increase/decrease over the eight years:

0FT/0PT -- 14.5% (+7.1)	0FT/ 1 PT – 16.6% (+5.5)	1FT/0PT – 9.9% (-5.6)
1FT/+1PT – 35.2% (+0.2)	2FT/0PT – 5.2% (-4.4)	2FT/+1 PT – 18.7% (-3.1)[8]

In essence, the number of congregations with part-time employees grew while those with full-time employees shrank, across the board. These figures are consistent with those in the other two groups as well, leading to the conclusion of a general decline in full-time compensated staff across all Canadian Christian churches. What is not explicit from their reporting is whether these numbers refer to all staff (including administrative, music, custodial, etc.) or purely pastoral and program positions. However, given the rest of their article, we are assuming the latter.

From their mid-decade study, the authors raise a few conclusions that we want to bring forward to interrogate along with the data from our study. In summary:

1. The percentage of part-time staff is increasing, likely pointing to shrinking budgets.

2. There are "good jobs" providing good salaries, benefits, and intrinsic/non-material rewards that are primarily found in large, urban congregations. There are "bad jobs" clustered in small, rural, poorer congregations. "Good job performance" is rewarded by moving to larger settings. There are certainly "good" pastors in "bad" jobs!

3. The data does not reveal the gender of those in the different employment categories, but, working from other data, they presume that women are over-represented in "bad" jobs in the church as well.[9] They note an increase in female and second-career clergy "who are willing to take part-time positions."

4. The move to part-time staffing has important denominational and congregational implications.

5. Mainline Protestants are least likely to have full-time staff and are most likely to have part-time and non-compensated staff.[10]

As we explore the questions of "part-time" and "bi-vocational" ministry, it quickly becomes apparent that even the language is contested. Most clergy who are remunerated for less than a 40-hour week, reject the term *part-time*. Don't call us part-time is their demand! And both the literature and this study confirm that. Regardless of the number of hours in the call or appointment, clergy consider themselves to be fully the minister of the community of faith. For that reason, in this study, part-time is strictly a reference to the number of hours remunerated per week according to the call or appointment form. There is no intention to refer to the number of hours actually worked – which is one of the foci of this study.

Bi-vocational is also a debated term. It seems to be uniquely applied to those employed in church settings. Thus, a teacher or mechanic who has a second job is rarely labeled bi-vocational, unless the second job is in ministry. Another term coming into use is "multi-vocational", recognizing that clergy who have a second job may indeed have more than two.[11]

Vocation, in church circles, generally refers to an invitation, call, or nudging by the divine, with a response similar to, "Here I am!" (Genesis 22: 1; Exodus 3: 4; 1 Samuel 3: 4; Isaiah 6: 8, etc.). The term bi-vocational could then mean more than one call in a single life or two jobs, one secular and one sacred. Usually, it is employed in the latter fashion; one ministry and one where the individual makes money. If we refer to "bi-vocational ministry" then, should the second/other job be pastoral in nature?

"Most of us find that « Part-time » is not accurate. Most of us work full-time, or close to full-time hours for part-pay. How do we make the shift to truly part-time and help congregations to understand what part-time means? Many people in our congregations do not realize how much work goes into ministry - for example prep for on-line worship. How can we help change that?" –Workshop participant

In one sense, bi-vocational ministry would apply to all Christians, regardless of status or employment. The concept of the priesthood of all believers stands on the premise that Christians are doing other things as well as fulfilling their discipleship. Sometimes this is referred to as *diakonia*. As a further step, however, bi-vocational is often applied to people who are undertaking jobs seen to be disconnected from the role of pastoral leader: "Tentmaking, bivocational, and multivocational are all terms currently used to describe how people who are involved in congregational leadership and work outside the congregation can combine those worlds."[12]

Uni-vocational ministry is certainly the norm within the United Church of Canada. While it is not explicitly stated anywhere, the prevailing assumption is that ministry is full-time. As recently as the 2010 edition of the *United Church Manual*,[13] one could find the expectation stated thusly: "The intention . . . is clearly that the member of the Order of Ministry be devoted to ministry," and, "When a member of the Order of Ministry is not willing to be devoted to the work of the ministry. . ."[14] disciplinary action could follow. At certain points in the denomination's history, this attitude was used to argue that first, all women, and then married women, were unsuitable for ordered ministry because they were presumed to have husbands and children that would distract them from this full devotion! While those debates no longer rage, the expectation of ministry as both a full-time vocation *and* a full-time job still widely predominates.[15]

While such wording does not specifically require full-time ministry from clergy, it reinforces the prior assumption and then pushes the point somewhat further by requiring ministers engaged in other (non-church) employment to seek annual approval and granting the judicatory authority to decide what is and is not "suitable". Such persons were listed in official documents as "retained on the roll" of clergy. In the current structure (effective January 1, 2019) there is no equivalent of that process. Instead, it is up to the Office of Vocation to certify that clergy are "in good standing" and that does not appear to relate to employment.

As a result, we might conclude that, institutionally at least, the United Church is becoming more open to part-time ministry. It has been several decades since arguments were made against the ordination of married women and women with children on the grounds that they would be unable to fully devote themselves to ministry (due to the assumed childcare requirements). However, the results of the survey reveal that many of those in part-time calls or appointments still feel a stigma attached to their status. This is by no means a reflection on the quality of their ministry or the appreciation of their congregations. It is, however, the fully employed, uni-vocational minister who is the starting point for most reflection on ministry and the standard against which clergy employment is judged and the health of congregations evaluated.

"Presbytery and Conference [judicatory bodies], however, seemed to be suspicious of me. They seemed to suspect my motivation." – Claire

Thus, the predominant image is of a minister serving a congregation or charge full-time. Unlike the situation in the United States, where so-called yoked congregations are sometimes offered as a solution both to clergy shortages and part-time ministry, multi-point pastoral charges have been a common structure within the United Church since the beginning.[16] If we were seeking consistency of language, we might refer to that as "bi-congregational" or "multi-congregational" ministry. Bi-vocational refers to a situation where the minister is employed by a congregation *and* another entity (paid or unpaid). For the purposes of this study, we have included within bi-vocational the emerging pattern of *cooperative* ministry, where a single individual holds a distinct call or appointment to more than one community of

"Ministry personnel serving multi-point charge and collaborative ministries face very similar challenges as part-time situations." - Workshop participant

faith. In those situations, there is commonly little or no organizational connection between the congregations. Regardless, the fully employed, uni-vocational minister is the starting point for most reflection on ministry and the standard against which clergy employment is judged.

The United Church has opened the door to a rethinking these traditional stances with the reception of the report, "Ministry Leadership to Meet the Needs of the Church in the 2020s."[17] Although it is not heralded as such, one of the key statements in the report comes in the second paragraph:

> After extensive consultation over eighteen months, the task group concludes that it is not reasonable to assume that every pastoral charge can have a pastorate without interruption (Basis of Union Section 10.10.2) as it might have been imagined or intended in 1925.[18]

The complete section reads:

> 10.2 The policy of the Church shall be that, as far as reasonably possible, every Pastoral Charge shall have a pastorate without interruption, and that, as far as reasonably possible, every effective member of the Order of Ministry shall have a Pastoral Charge or Community of Faith.[19]

By acknowledging that a fundamental understanding of the relationship between church and clergy is no longer sustainable, the report opens the door to a much wider discussion of the nature of ministry to which we will return.

Bi-vocational implies having more than one source of income. For the purposes of this study, we have expanded that definition to include a second *job* which may or may not be paid. This allows us to incorporate the reality that many individuals feel a *call* or *vocation* to an activity regardless of pay. While this may complicate the picture, we feel it is the only way to honestly reflect the perspective of those who participated in the study. Thus, we have in mind the following loose categories:

- Full-time bi-vocational: an individual in a full-time call or appointment who engages in another pursuit for a significant time each week (paid or unpaid)
- Willingly bi-vocational, part-time: those in less than full-time call or appointment by choice, in order that they have the significant time for another pursuit each week (paid or unpaid)
- Unwillingly bi-vocational: those in less than full-time call or appointment who either from necessity or responsibility devote significant time for another pursuit each week (paid or unpaid)
- Unwillingly part-time: those in less than full-time call or appointment who would prefer to be in full-time ministry if circumstances permitted.

Thus, we see that an easy reference to "part-time ministry" hides as much as it clarifies.

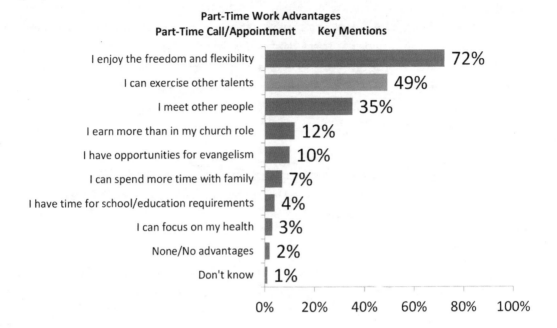

Follow the Money

Growth in part-time ministry can be directly linked to the demographic and societal factors impacting the United Church (and other formerly mainline traditions) over the decades. At one point, the denomination had congrega-

But honestly, if I didn't have money in the bank in investments making income, this would not be sustainable for me."- Roberta

tions in virtually every community, many of them smaller and rural. Rural depopulation and a shift in church attendance patterns across the generations translated into decreased human and financial resources. This is coupled with generally poor (comparatively) financial steward-ship levels. Until approximately fifteen years ago some support was available to financially struggling congregations from the denomination. However, as national funds shrank, an intentional shift occurred directing such monies as were available away from congregations to other forms of mission and outreach. Participants in these congregations often work tirelessly to raise funds for their own ministry and to generously address needs in the community but rising costs and a shrinking population base create a situation where reduction in ministry is often seen as the only response.

The United Church operates on a salary scale established by the General Council that pre-scribes minimum amounts and experience-based incremental increases.[20] That salary scale also incorporates cost of living based amounts for housing (grounded in real estate prices in differ-ent places in the national market). Similarly, with health benefits, pension contributions, study and travel allowances, vacation, and continuing education time, there are established minimums. This salary scale does a great deal to avoid some of the exploitative employment practices encountered in other churches. It also provides congregations with very clear financial parameters.

Another trend impacting part-time ministry is the shift away from church-owned housing. Thirty years ago, most congregations owned a manse or parsonage. Today that number is 10% and not all of those are available for clergy housing because they are rented as a source of congregational income. There is plenty of scope to debate the results of that change for congregations and clergy! One effect that impacts the choices of part-time congregations is that, with the increase in housing costs across Canada and a dearth of suitable options in many smaller communities, the costs of relocating are prohibitive. This means that congregations are restricted to those ministers already living within a commuting distance. As a corollary, the absence of church-owned housing increases the monthly cash-flow demands on congregations providing a salary since it must include a housing amount.

Unlike some traditions with a more robust and developed practice and theology of bi-vocational ministry, there is no situation in the United Church (at least officially) where someone serves a congregation without pay. Since the denomination works from a central payroll source, there is only marginal opportunity for non-stipendiary congregational leadership. On the other hand, there are anecdotal accounts of clergy either being pressured to or volunteering to give back a portion of their remuneration. We can conclude that full-time and part-time clergy are treated according to the same financial standards, qualified only by the number of hours employed.

"When I was living in a manse and doing part time ministry prior to comprehensive salary I was doing okay financially but since coming to my new pastoral charge, without a manse, my part-time ministry salary goes 2/3 towards housing leaving 1/3 to raise a family with three children. I know I can't keep this up financially even though this is the ministry I want to do and that works for my family. So... that's disheartening."
- Workshop participant

"Once I stopped working full-time within the church and had an interest outside of it, I feel that I was a much better minister. My preaching improved because of some of the classes I took for my [other] degree. My awareness of First Nations issues, my writing ability, I can remember specific classes that I felt, "wow, I wish I'd had these before I served in ministry."- Claire

The bi-vocational minister is more than simply a lay volunteer. They are trained, credentialled and overseen by the church. They are accountable to the denomination through the Office of Vocation. Except for those in cooperative or shared ministries, bi-vocational clergy blur the lines between sacred and secular, moving back and forth on a regular basis.

Bi-vocational employment can mean divided loyalties as will be explored further in this study. One judicatory task force specifically pointed out the connection between finances and accountability: "Bivocationality is the arrangement in which a pastor spends time and energy working for compensation and is accountable to another in addition to the setting in which s/he has been called to minister"[21]

As our research indicates, there is a significant (and seemingly growing) cadre of pastors who are fully committed to bi-vocational ministry. Intentional bi-vocationalism (what we refer to as willingly bi-vocational) is beginning to gain traction as a concept. It includes different assumptions and different conclusions about church structure and ministry.[22] In some cases, the question is not about the congregation's ability or inability to pay a full-time salary. Instead, by mutual agreement (or the desire of the individual), there is less than full-time employment. In other studies, clergy report that financial independence "empowers their ministry" and allows them to take risks.[23]

A Wider View of Bi-Vocational

Bi-vocational ministry can be an intentional missional and vocational strategy, although we may need to step outside our recent practices to understand it. The incarnational aspect of ministry by a pastor and congregation engaged

> "I can do ministry in different ways, especially with non-church folk"
> - Marlene

in work outside the walls of the church also allows them to connect with folks they would not otherwise be able to reach.[24] In some contexts, such as extreme secularization[25] or in countries that restrict evangelism,[26] working a secular job is a cross cultural missional strategy, though "overseas" tentmaking is sometimes distinguished from other forms of bi-vocational ministry.[27] This option is of particular importance to church planters, who cannot count on a salary from a fledgling congregation. The term *co-vocational* is sometimes used to identify a situation in which "the pastor's calling and ministry occur in a traditionally non-pastoral setting," such as a church planter running a coffee shop as a ministry.[28] For these and other bi-vocational ministers, the secular job is also ministry: "Tentmakers witness with their whole lives and their jobs are integral to their work for the Kingdom of God."[29] This whole-life witness evidences integration of one's multiple vocations. Integration can contribute to successful and healthy ministry.

Rather than being second-class or undesirable, bi-vocational ministry has the potential to positively impact a congregation's understanding of its own vocation. Even if driven by finances, such ministry, approached intentionally, can spark a renaissance in the congregation's life. It is not uncommon for congregations to expect the minister to "do" most of the ministry. In part-time situations, those ministries must be shared if they are to occur. Creativity, ingenuity, and experimentation open the possibility for parishioners to explore unused gifts and callings. Intentionally reflecting on bi-vocational ministry can lead the congregation to understand that the ministry is truly theirs and the clergy's role is to assist them to live it out. This has always been the case, but it is easier to ignore when there is a full-timer around to do the lifting! Approached intentionally, the full range of the congregation's ministry can be grist for theological reflection and for "the people of God" to find their calling. That will require the denomination to be far more deliberate in its approach to part-time ministry and encouraging a different approach to a community's call. Bi-vocational ministry can encourage whole new ways of envisioning the church

The bi-vocational pastor becomes part of a leadership team, and not necessarily the shining star. That role change demands something of clergy too, who by their training and experience may have fallen into taking on all (or the most important) ministry tasks. Are they willing to give those up, and not just the ones they'd prefer to avoid?

One concern raised about bi-vocational ministry is that of divided loyalties. A judicatory task force specifically pointed out the connection between finances and accountability: "Bivocationality is the arrangement in which a pastor spends time and energy working for compensation and is accountable to another in addition to the setting in which s/he has been called to minister."[30] This raises very real issues in the management of such a ministry. To what extent if at all, does the other employment allow the minister to respond to pastoral emergencies or alter work responsibilities to engage in ministry activities? For instance, is the minister able to attend at the time of death or schedule a funeral for any day desired, or are they restricted by their other commitment? This cuts two ways: if there are restrictions, how understanding is the congregation of their minister's reality and is there someone to step up for the ministry? On the other hand, if the minister has a great deal of latitude in their other employment, to what extent does ministry intrude into that time, providing the congregation with a false sense of what part-time ministry really represents?

"One of the realities is that people feel that you are full-time. My congregation doesn't, but it's often [from people in the community] who ask? Why can't you do this? Why isn't your church doing more than this?' Often, it's people who don't understand or family members of the church people." – Roberta

In one of the [candidacy process] interviews, a member of the team had been bivocational and she was encouraging [to me], although she said it was difficult and at that point she was focusing on full-time ministry. [That] hasn't been common to hear of it.

In another interview, when she indicated that she wasn't done with her other work a team members (ordained) said "Something's got to give," which she interpreted as being, you need to choose. It felt like a judgement statement: if you're not all in you're not in it." - Barbara

I. Ross Bartlett

QUESTIONS FOR DISCUSSION

1. Have you ever been employed part-time? Was that by choice or circumstance? What was that experience like for you?

2. What advantages and disadvantages can you list for part-time ministry? For the congregation? For the minister?

3. If your congregation's minister was part-time, what would you hope their weekly priority(s) would be?

4. If you are (or were) a congregational minister, would you prefer part-time or full-time ministry? What are some of the factors influencing your choice?

ENDNOTES

[1] Sam Reimer, Rick Hiemstra, "The Rise of Part-time Employment in Canadian Christian Churches", *Studies in Religion,* 2015, Volume 43(3), 356-377.

[2] R.W. Bibby, *Beyond the Gods and Back: Religion's Demise and Rise and Why It Matters,* (Lethbridge; Canada Project Books, 2011).

[3] Reimer and Hiemstra, "The Rise", 358, citing J Wallace, *Part-time Work in Canada:Report of the Commission into Part-time Work in Canada,* Ottawa, Supply and Services, 1983 and Stats Canada 2013, Employment by sex and age group.

[4] Reimer and Hiemstra, "The Rise", 358-9.

[5] J. Carroll, *God's Potters: Pastoral Leadership and the Shaping of Congregations,* (Grand Rapids; Eerdman's, 2006).

[6] Reimer and Heimstra, "The Rise", citing Bibby, *Beyond.*

[7] United Church of Canada (1,073 congregations), Anglican Church of Canada (647), Presbyterian Church in Canada (366), Evangelical Lutheran Church (346), Others (360).

[8] Reimer and Heimstra, "The Rise", 363, Table 1.

[9] The authors make no mention of gender-fluid and LGBTQ clergy as identifiable groups.

[10] Reimer and Heimstra, "The Rise," 367-70.

[11] Watson et al, *Canadian Multivocational Ministry Project,* Toronto, 2020.

[12] Watson et al. 2020, p. 3.

[13] *The United Church Manual,* multiple editions, is the governance document for the denomination.

[14] *Manual,* United Church of Canada, 2010, sect 314 (4) and 314 (5i)

[15] The explicit references to "devoted to ministry" do not appear in editions of *The Manual* after 2010.

[16] See the Appendix of an explanation of denominational structures.

[17] United Church of Canada, "Ministry Leadership to Meet the Needs of the Church in the 20202s" received by the General Council Executive, November 19, 2020 accessible at https://unitedchurch. sharepoint.com/:w:/r/sites/UnitedChurchCommons/_layouts/15/Doc.aspx?sourcedoc=%7B-557F3F8D-17BF-4AE5-A749-DD4448D0C0B8%7D&file=Ministry%20Leadership%20to%20 Meet%20the%20Needs%20of%20the%20Church%20in%20the%202020s%20Report%20FINAL. docx&action=default&mobileredirect=true. (Accessed January 14, 2022)

[18] "Ministry Leadership", 1.

[19] United Church of Canada, *The Manual,* 2022, Basis of Union, section 10.10.2. The Basis of Union is the foundational constitutional document of the denomination. All other aspects of the church's life flow from there.

[20] See for example, United Church of Canada, Minimum Salaries & Reimbursements for Ministry Personnel (2021) https://united-church.ca/sites/default/files/2021-salary-schedule-ministry-personnel.pdf. Accessed November 30, 2021.

[21] Christian Reformed Church in North America 2020, p. 11.

[22] Mark D. W Edington, *Bivocational: Returning to the Roots of Ministry*. (New York: Church Publishing). Available online: http://www.bivocational.church/ (accessed on 11 January 2021), 8.

[23] Kristen Plinke Bentley, "Perspectives of Bi-Vocational Ministry: Emerging Themes in Bi-Vocational Ministry Research at Lexington Theological Seminary", *Lexington Theological Quarterly* 48: 115–51. Available online: https://www.lextheo.edu/wp-content/ uploads/2019/10/j-4-Perspectives-of-Bi-Voca-tional-Ministry.pdf (accessed on 11 January 2021),129.

[24] Christian Reformed Church in North America 2020, p. 17; Mark, D. W. Edington, Bivocational: Returning to the Roots of Ministry. New York: Church p. 14; Watson et al., p. 15.

[25] James W Watson and Narry F. Santos, "Tentmaking: Creative Mission Opportunities within a Secularizing Canadian Society", *in* Narry F. Santos and Mark Naylor (eds.) *Mission and Evangelism in a Secularizing World*: Academy, Agency, and Assembly Perspectives from Canada, Evangelical Missiological Society Monograph Series 2. Eugene: Pickwick, 2019, 139.

[26] Forum for World Evangelization, "The Local Church in Mission", Lausanne Occasional Paper No. 39, 2004, sec. 3.1 Available online:
https://www.lausanne.org/content/lop/local-church-mission-lop-39#cpb (accessed January 12 2022); Global Connections," The Challenge of Tentmaking, Serving God through One's Profession and Business Overseas," Available online: https://www.globalconnections.org.uk/sites/newgc.localhost/files/papers/The%20Challenge%20of%20Tentmaking.
pdf (accessed on January 12 2022).

[27] H.M.Samushonga, "On Bivocational Ministry-focused Training in British Theological Schools: Dialoguing with British Theological Educationalists", *Practical Theology, 13,387.*

[28] Christian Reformed Church in North America 2020, pp. 11–12).

[29] Forum for World Evangelism, "The Local Church."

[30] Christian Reformed Church in North America, "Study of Bivocationality Task Force. October 30," 2020, 11. Available online: https: //www.faithaliveresources.org/Products/830135/study-of-bivoca-tionality-task-force.aspx (accessed on 11 January 2021).

Part-time Ministry and the Congregation

Currently, most congregations that move to part-time ministry do so as a result of declining resources. As a result, the move is often accompanied by feelings of diminishment and failure. In order to receive part-time ministry as the gift it is, we need to probe our assumptions about congregational well-being. That's the focus of this chapter.

How important is the numerical size of a congregation in considering vitality, vibrancy, and faithfulness? How do we attempt to measure such factors? Discussing it may make us uncomfortable, but such judgements occur when we decide which communities of faith will be supported and when we judge what real or fully committed ministry looks like. The current practice gives de facto authority to a market-based approach to congregational survival: if a congregation lacks sufficient customers (congregants) then it lessens the services (ministry) it provides. Which is akin to a company seeking to stave off bankruptcy by cutting sales and service personnel! However, is the size of budget, membership, attendance, or any similar factor a useful predictor of effectiveness, longevity, and faithfulness? Is the broader mission of the church served by the diminishing (and closure) of small communities of faith? Phrased another way, how do these qualities correlate to the capacity to provide employment?

> "I think people need a sacred place in the community. The place is important. How do we maintain sacred spaces? If sharing with another denomination is what it takes to keep an identified space in your community, then so be it." - *Andrea*

One response to the growth of part-time calls/appointments would have the wider church compel congregations to work together to provide full-time employment. While the judicatories (Regions) have the authority to do so (through the power of withholding authorization for part-time vacancies) experience suggests that this is dangerous road. In past instances when congregations have been compelled to do something the results have not always been positive and it is the clergy, as the frontline representatives of the church, who bear the brunt of any displeasure. So, while it is certainly within the power and the authority of the wider church to not approve part-time vacancies, making such a policy healthy and effective would require an investment in skills, resources, and people to do the work of institutional change management within the communities of faith being combined.

Cooperative ministries (those situations where a clergyperson receives multiple calls and/or appointments at the same time from two or more different communities of faith) offer another possible solution to the lack of a living wage. However, unless some intentional energy goes into revising the governance structure, the burden in such settings is generally carried by the ministry personnel. As a result, in multiple part-time situations (although they may have full employment), clergy still lack the time to foster the tasks of visioning, equipping, outreach, and evangelism. It would also require clarity and fortitude on the part of judicatories and their committees to determine the response when a community of faith comes forward with someone who genuinely desires a part-time ministry appointment. How will they account for the approval of a part-time vacancy in one part of the area while insisting that communities of faith cooperate to create a full-time vacancy in others?

Mainline church leaders have been anxious about declining membership numbers for more than fifty years. The faster the apparent decline the more extreme the rhetoric. Currently, "vital congregations" is the most widely used terminology.[1]

> "The vision of vital congregations and the need for more churches to live up to that term is washing across the beaches of all denominations." Herb Miller, 1990

One of the first studies of "congregational vitality" was undertaken by the Presbyterian Church in Canada in the 1970s through a committee whose name signaled the ambitious goal of doubling church membership within the decade.[2] It was soon joined by a multitude of studies from most of the mainline denominations and other faith groups. This fulfilled the prediction of church consultant Herb Miller (1990): "The vision of vital congregations and the need for more churches to live up to that term is washing across the beaches of all denominations,"[3] Many of these studies revealed that the reasons for decline were complex and mixed institutional, social, and demographic forces. In other words, they would not respond to quick and easy programmatic or leadership fixes.

One potent response to the demographic and social changes impacting the Christian land-scape in North America came through the "church growth movement." Dean Kelley's book, *Why Conservative Churches are Growing* (1972)[4] brought wide attention to the movement begun by Donald McGavran at the Fuller Seminary School of World Missions. Over the years a vast treasury of resources, books, and papers, paralleled by the growth of evangelical mega-churches, was driven by the foundational assumptions that numerical growth is a prime measurement of congregational faithfulness and, the church can best accomplish that goal through carefully focusing on a demographic chosen according to racial, socio-economic, age and other factors and shaping all aspects of life to attract such a group.[5]

While there was much for the mainline to learn from the church growth movement, many aspects were simply inconsistent with mainline self-understanding and theology. The mainline challenge was not planting new congregations, (as many such denominations were represented in most jurisdictions) but reviving "ailing" congregations.[6] By 2000, "vitality" had become the default language in many denominations, covering virtually every aspect of congregational health and growth. Much of that emphasis is summarized in the book, *Five Practices of Fruitful Congregations*[7], which has enjoyed wide popularity within the United Church of Canada. United Methodist Bishop Robert Schnase presents an approachable and user-friendly guide focusing on radical hospitality, passionate worship, intentional faith development, risk-taking mission and service, and extravagant generosity. There are echoes of these themes in many different places and programs. However, it could well be argued that the effective metrics of vitality in the United Church remain primarily numerical, membership/participation and financial.

Measurements of vitality based primarily on numbers (membership and finances) place many part-time congregations in a no-win situation. While there is always a place for genuine hospitality and sharing the life of faith, the simple reality is that many congregations have come to their current place, at least in part, as a result of out-migration. At the turn of the century, it was popularly estimated that two-thirds of the congregations were rural and two-thirds of the membership was urban/suburban. Current data suggests little change. However, the rural/town membership is spread over a larger number of communities. For such congregations it would be helpful to pair Schnase's hopeful

Location	Congregation	Membership
City/suburban	31.2%	41.9%
Rural/town	68.8%	58.1%

United Church of Canada, Information and Statistics (January 2022)

text with Loren Mead's, *More than Numbers: The Ways Churches Grow*.[8] Mead explored what church growth and evangelism really mean in a time when it is mathematically impossible for every congregation to achieve significant numerical growth. He argued provocatively that spiritual, organizational, and missional growth are just as important as numerical growth, and that all four are needed for a truly healthy and growing church. Such congregations and their leaders might also benefit from considering Peter Steinke, *Congregational Leadership in Anxious Times: Being Calm and Courageous No Matter What*.[9] He reminds us that congregations, just like individuals, cannot thrive when focused on survival alone.

Understanding Ministry

How does the denomination understand ministry, particularly in the sense of a genuinely part-time and/or bi-vocational call? Our survey and interviews uncovered a feeling of being misunderstood and harshly judged amongst some

"It needs to be acknowledged and normalized. It's not the exception. I don't see how we can avoid it."
- Andrea

part-timers. Many of these folk prefer and feel called to part-time ministry. It is an open question whether the church would enjoy their services were they compelled to undertake full-time pastoral ministry. Some clearly indicate that full-time is not possible for them. Within this part-time group, there is a subgroup who feel quite committed to their bi-vocational status. For these individuals, their non-pastoral work is a ministry in the fullest sense of the word. Can the church broaden its sense of ministry to accommodate them?

Concurrently, there is also growing group of clergy who are dissatisfied with their part-time situation. Since these folk are predominantly in the most recently credentialled (who as a cluster have been shown to generally experience higher degrees of disenchantment) what can the denomination do to sustain and better support them? This connects to the question of the awareness of candidates for ministry about their employment prospects. In a quick poll of M.Div. students, both in-community and on-campus programs, only 20% could recall anyone speaking of part-time ministry, either in their candidacy process or education. The students were about evenly divided in their anticipation of full-time ministry employment following ordination. However, 56% acknowledged considering bi-vocational ministry (defined for this instance as "working part-time in pastoral ministry and part-time in another role"). None of the students could recall any training or education specific to a part-time ministry vocation, but 79% would welcome such a focus. This is consistent with the responses from Office of Vocation ministers, Candidacy Board chairs, and academic heads of various institutions involved in clergy training. Our interviews with survey respondents revealed a number of things that people wished they had known prior to engaging in part-time ministry. These range from better help in setting boundaries and scheduling, to financial literacy, and resources for dealing with employment insecurity.

> Candidate responses:
>
> 20% recall someone speaking about part-time
>
> 50% anticipate full-time ministry
>
> 56% are open to considering bi-vocational
>
> 79% welcome more emphasis on part-time in their education.

Is it time to re-think ministry?

The survey and interviews confirmed a trend that appears in the literature. For part-time ministry to be effective we must recognize that

> It's time to end the myth of the complete leader; the flawless person at the top who's got it all figured out. In fact, the sooner leaders stop trying to be all things to all people, the better off their organizations will be.[10]

Although these words are found in a prominent business journal, they apply equally to congregations and especially to those entering part-time ministry – as well as to their clergy! As we have seen, the historically anomalous growth of full-time professional clergy throughout the nineteenth and twentieth centuries sidelined a much deeper tradition of clergy and laity working together in a shared ministry model. Earlier we acknowledged that the understood view of laity as consumers of ministry provided by clergy was a block to vital part-time ministry. Now we must turn the light on clergy and ask the related question: to what extent does clergy self-perception as professional generalist providers of quality ministry hamper the vitality of part-time settings?

The twentieth century saw an unprecedented expansion of seminaries and theological schools, training centres and specialty departments related to various aspects of ministry practice. In significant measure that growth was predicated on and fueled by the expectation that there would predominantly be full-time clergy in congregations and that individuals would step forward to take up those student spots on the way to professional ministry. Although there are many and valid critiques to be made of the mainline church in the last century for the most part that model worked for the involved clergy and laity. A tremendous amount of good and faithful ministry happened and happens today. Questioning the historically unique model is in no sense intended to cast doubt on the sincerity or effectiveness of any of the participants. However, if the context has changed (as the shrinking of the mainline church and the growth of part-time ministries would seem to indicate) can the same model and the commitments it fostered be sustained? We need to acknowledge some challenges from the beginning.

The United Church has had, since its inception, a stated goal that, within reason, every minister shall be employed:

> The policy of the Church shall be that, as far as reasonably possible, every
> Pastoral Charge shall have a pastorate without interruption, and that, as far
> as reasonably possible, every effective member of the Order of Ministry shall
> have a Pastoral Charge or Community of Faith. [11]

In a move that could signal a major shift in our understanding of ministry, a very recent task group report reads, in part: "[I]t is not reasonable to assume that every pastoral charge can have a pastorate without interruption as it might have been imagined or intended in 1925."[12] Regardless of what may actually have been happening throughout the decades, making such a change in the fundamental self-understanding of what ministry is and how it is exercised represents an enormous shift.

There are some communities of faith whose season has passed and those where there is no desire or energy to change received patterns. They were, perhaps for some considerable period, vibrant and vital congregations doing important and faithful work. However, whatever the series of circumstances that brings us to today, the current membership lacks the energy or vision to undertake what would be necessary to turn the corner to new life. One symptom of that is the fantasy that the perfect minister will somehow create a revival and the bias that says the minister should do it all because that's what we pay them for. While such a conclusion should not be arrived at hastily it is also appropriate that, when it is evident, such a season should be honoured, celebrated, and ministered to in appropriate ways. While some situations may be ripe for replanting (see below) many are not and for the wider church to participate in such an illusion is cruel and deceptive and sometimes involves the active misleading of candidates for vacancies (for instance, when the revenues available to sustain ministry are actively misstated during the search process).

There are part-time clergy, not all of them retired or semi-retired, who have no real incentive to change the trajectory of their congregation(s). They have come to a place in their journey of discipleship where pastoring a smaller and slowly dwindling community is the extent of their passion for ministry. That service should not be scorned. However, the life of a congregation should not be subject to the limitations of the clergy and, if potential for positive change is seen in a particular location, honest effort needs to be made to facilitate a more appropriate realignment of resources and needs.

At some point we must also tackle the ticklish and challenging subject of clergy themselves and their own motivations. This is a sensitive subject because it is easy to mistake it for criticism. *That is not the intention!* However, the attitudes and behaviours of clergy can well make or break a part-time pastorate. A joyful part-time pastor delights in seeing congregants discover a love and gift for ministry arts, including those long-believed to be the province of clergy. The church – congregations, judicatories, training practices – have all conspired to promote the myth of the complete leader. "Only when

> *"I used to be neurotically responsible, and when you're in part-time ministry you have to be able to let go and not worry if something goes wrong." - Catherine*

leaders come to see themselves as incomplete – as having both strengths and weaknesses - will they be able to make up for their missing skills by relating to others."[13] In order to staff for success, an effort must be made to gauge the temperament of the minister in this crucial sphere. That's one reason why those who do not feel called to part-time ministry should not be compelled to undertake it. The effective part-time minister must have a high degree of self-awareness that sometimes they are not the best at every task. Many different leadership styles can be used at different points but collaborative and enabling must be readily available to the minister.[14] The part-time minister must avoid colluding with the learned helplessness of the congregation. As one interviewee put it:" Sometimes people don't want to be set free."

At some point, a moral issue must be wrestled with. In the dominant existing understanding, ministry is full-time and lifelong. As we have seen, a significant proportion of those preparing for ministry cannot recall any discussion or preparation for alternative models. However, if the church is aware of the shifting employment landscape what obligations does it have to its primary employees? After all, pastoral employment in all situations must be sanctioned by the church (through the process of approving calls/appointments). Certainly, individual agency applies to clergy accepting part-time roles. It is worth asking, however, what if any,

> *"There needs to be better financial watchdog to make sure that the welfare is looked after. The system is still geared to full-time." - Andrea*

responsibility the church bears when it approves such employment, knowing that the remuneration will not cover repayment on loans taken to achieve the credentialling required for employment? This is especially pressing when we are aware that the number of full-time positions is dwindling. What is the moral covenant of the church with its largest group of employees?

Dream with us for a moment and picture a situation where the church could honour equally those who are called to a life of full-time pastoral ministry and those who are also called, but to expressions of ministry which are both congregationally and otherwise expressed. Imagine a situation where clergy and congregations could lay down the burdens of guilt or failure that they carry for not living out society's norms of success and, instead, recognize the good fruits of their shared ministry for what they are. Think of the possibilities that emerge when a congregation (regardless of size) sees the ministry as belonging to them and are joined by clergy who have a vocation to equip and encourage others. Those are the challenges and promises of part-time ministry that we will explore more fully in the next chapter.

QUESTIONS FOR DISCUSSION

1. How would you describe a vital or faithful congregation? Do those words mean something different to you? What emphasis would you place on numbers (members or revenue) in your description?

2. If a congregation cannot grow numerically (perhaps because of community demographics) what are other forms of faithful growth?

3. The text suggests that many congregations have fallen into a consumer/producer model of ministry, dependent on clergy. Do you think this is fair? How would you characterize a healthy minister-congregation relationship?

ENDNOTES

[1] Darryl Stephens, "Healing Congregations: A Corrective to the Metrics of Congregational Vitality." *Witness: Journal of the Academy for Evangelism in Theological* Education Volume 34 (2020) https://journals.sfu.ca/witness/index.php/witness Accessed November 30, 2021.

[2] Presbyterian Church in Canada, National Committee for Church Growth, "Soundings of Congregational Vitality: The Presbyterian Church in Canada 1976–1980, National Research Project of the Presbyterian Church in Canada,
Committee on Church Growth to Double in the Eighties", (Ontario: Don Mills, 1981), cited Stephens, "Healing".

[3] Herb Miller, *The Vital Congregation*, Effective Church Series, vol. 1 (Nashville: Abingdon 1990), 12.

[4] There is a story that Kelly's original title, *Why Strict Churches are Growing*, was changed by the publisher to have wider market appeal.

[5] C. Peter Wagner, *Your Church Can Grow* (Glendale:Regal, 1976), 159. One reviewer observed that "there is only a fine line between 'homogeneous unit' and racism": Val J. Sauer, "Review of Wagner, C Peter. Your Church Can Grow," *Foundations* 20 no. 2 (Apr–Jun 1977): 183–187. Cited in Stephens, "Healing", this comment encapsulates much mainline discomfort with the church growth movement's perceived willingness to exclude those who did not fit the desired target audience.

[6] In the early 2000s, the United Church hosted an event entitled "More Franchises", playing with the idea that there were more congregations than iconic Tim Horton's shops in the land.

[7] Robert Schnase, http://robertschnase.com/books/fivepractices-of-fruitful-congregations/; Robert Schnase, Five Practices of Fruitful Congregations: Revised and Updated (Nashville: Abingdon, 2018).

[8] Mead, Loren B. *More than Numbers: The Ways Churches Grow*. (Washington, D.C.: Alban Institute, 1993). Alban Institute Publication; AL 141.

[9] Peter L. Steinke, *Congregational Leadership in Anxious Times: Bering Calm and Courageous No Matter What*, (Herndon, VA: Alban Institute, 2006), 15–17.

[10] D Acona, T Malone, W. Orlikowski and P Senge, "In Praise of the Incomplete Leader", *Harvard Business Review*, 85 (2), 110 cited in Arthur Rank Centre for Rural Ministries, "Leadership and ministry, lay and ordained: insights from rural multi-church groups Summary Report," University of Derby, 2019, pg 1. Accessible at https://arthurrankcentre.org.uk/resources/leadership-and-ministry-lay-and-ordained-insights-for-rural-multi-church-groups-summary-report/ Accessed January 14, 2022.

[11] *Manual* 2019, Polity section, 10.2.

[12] United Church of Canada, "Ministry Leadership to meet the Needs of the Church in the 2020s," presented to the General Council Executive, November, 19-20, 2021, 1. Found at https://unitedchurch.sharepoint.com/:w:/r/sites/UnitedChurchCommons/_layouts/15/Doc.aspx?source-doc=%7B557F3F8D-17BF-4AE5-A749-DD4448D0C0B8%7D&file=Ministry%20Leadership%20to%20Meet%20the%20Needs%20of%20the%20Church%20in%20the%202020s%20Report%20FINAL.docx&action=default&mobileredirect=true Accessed January 5, 2022.

[13] Acona, "In Praise", 10.

[14] Arthur Rank, "Leadership", 9.

Exploring Possibilities

If you've come this far on the journey, you're ready to think about other possibilities for ministry in mainline congregations. Let's review

- There is a long and honourable history of part-time ministry in the Christian story that predates the twentieth century development of full-time norms
- There is theological grounding that makes bi-vocational more than just an administrative necessity
- In at least one mainline denomination there is documented evidence of a rapid and accelerating growth in part-time positions
- At the very least, this phenomenon invites our reconsideration of old assumptions about ministry

But can it go further? Can we move beyond grim necessity or fatalistic embracing of inevitable shrinkage and decline to see a gift of the Divine? We believe the answer is yes, but certain conditions will need to be met.

Bi-vocational or part-time ministry is practiced within communities of faith and the success (however measured) of such ministry is also dependent on the congregation. If a significant portion of the congregation is not committed to this expression of the church, it will be impossible for a vital spiritual life to emerge. Put bluntly, if those who expect ministry to be done "for them" by a full-time clergy person do not experience a radical shift in commitment to accept the reality of ministry done "by them," then part-time ministry will likely be the gateway to the dwindling and ending of the congregation's service, perhaps well before its time. Especially when the congregation is moving from full time to part-time call/appointment it is crucial for the lay members to adopt an attitude declaring that they can do it. They will probably need to be coached and guided into and through the new reality. Partly because of the absence of apparent options, many congregations default to a consumeristic mode and use finances as the primary/sole means of assessment.

Doing things differently implies a degree of planning/training/intentionality that is often absent now. The transition to part-time ministry is not an easy

"People need help to see the possibilities and get excited rather than simply lamenting the good old days" - Andrea

one. Several of our interviewees commented on that fact. When one is not the first part-timer, then the expectations and patterns have shifted over time. One interviewee noted the contrast in expectations between a longer-term part-time congregation and the newly part-time congregation which was now part of their cooperative ministry. The former group was much more respectful of boundaries and more limited availability. When the decision for part-time is driven primarily by finances rather than a sense of call many congregations put off the step until other options are exhausted (often along with the congregants). The possibilities of vital part-time ministry are not discussed for fear that such conversation will cause the very reality that is feared. They are like the individual who refuses to write a will thinking that it will bring about death! The result is a tragic

> *She has always been in part-time ministry, having been settled into one. She feels that when she began, she and her peers were told that this was the only way into ministry and, "after a while" there would be full-time work. That has never happened for her.*
> *- Roberta's experience.*

mess for those who come after. The community of faith crashes into part-time ministry largely unprepared for the reality and the wider church often compounds the problem by allowing the call/appointment of candidates or credentialled clergy with very limited experience into some of the most challenging ministry situations imaginable. As a result of the changes in the United Church Candidacy Pathway, Regions are seeking locations to serve as Supervised Ministry Experience sites with varying degrees of intentionality regarding the suitability of such places. Some congregations, having expended whatever financial reserves they may have had, have nothing to cushion the shock of change. How can we help congregations to get out in front moving to part-time when the shift can provide the greatest benefit?

Of course there are exceptions to the scenario just outlined, but they are rare. They generally occur when a community of faith has been able to courageously grasp a new vision of faithfulness; has been counselled or compelled to enter Intentional Interim ministry; has been able to secure the ministry of someone who capable of

> *"Because we are in part-time, the congregation has moved beyond survival mode" - Robert*

coaching them as they enter a new reality; or have called/appointed a minister who resolutely refuses to let them slip back into the old ways while encouraging new habits of ministry shared by all God's people.

Making those exceptions a more common reality demands several changes in process primarily having to do with intentional planning, clearly identifiable steps that congregations take so that they can discern the sort(s) of faithful ministry being called forth well before a part-time appointment or call is approved. The crucial initial step: having a plan and a

> *"What kind of support is there nationally and regionally to ensure that people aren't paid part time but are working full time to meet expectations?"*
> *- Workshop participant*

congregational commitment to enter the journey of part-time ministry. The expectation that the called or appointed minister will be some sort of hero who will do full-time work for part-time pay must be addressed and countered in concrete ways. The plan should include a commitment from the congregation concerning the parts of ministry they are prepared to undertake with support and training. This could expand to position descriptions, expected levels of training and clear expectations of the ways in which an incoming minister would support and enhance (but not do) their ministry.[1]

In fact, there are thriving part-time ministries within the United Church; in other words, communities of faith that are faithfully living into a sense of Divine invitation with joyful courage. These should be studied to provide examples of "life after full-time "and clarify certain common actions or decisions that appear in those cases and can be customize for each setting. These stories should be made available to judicatories as they work with communities of faith and to training institutions as they prepare candidates. Some of those vital congregations may find new ministries and increased self-worth by acting as coaching or training locations.

> "The congregation said: 'We don't think we can keep paying you. What do we need to do?' With Presbytery help they worked out funding for transitional ministry. Looking at the question: 'Who are we and, particularly, what is the role of money in our life as a people of God?'"- Andrea

Putting off hard decisions as long as possible is very human. As a result, judicatories may need to undertake proactive work with communities of faith before the moment of crisis. How can we assist congregations where part-time ministry is the foreseeable reality make appropriate decisions while still in some degree of health? This is good stewardship and planning as well as appropriate care for clergy who, where the shift to part-time is being resisted without creative response, often find themselves tremendously overburdened and drained. If part-time ministry (perhaps with a bi-vocational component) can be honoured and accepted as *good ministry,* it may even be possible for a well-loved and effective minister to stay and aid the transition instead of leaving to save themselves. Such a step would benefit from effective and supportive intervention from the local judicatory.

In an existing or newly emerging part-time ministry situation, congregants need to be encouraged and empowered to develop their particular gifts. Judicatories may need to be more intentional about providing resources, clergy better trained as coaches and teachers,

> "I don't think they should be allowing congregations to do what my congregation did, they were together as a full-time unit with another charge, and then they split the set. OK, that worked for the churches, but I don't know that in most situations it works out well for overall ministry. I think they need to look at saying, 'OK, we can't keep up all these little churches with tiny congregations.' I wish we had a bishop who would say, 'You three, you're together on the same team now!'" – Roberta

and congregations more supportive of their members. Many lay people have skills and experience that, with a little creative thought and supportive development, translate well to work in church world. As we've seen, in past generations they would have grown up in the church seeing an older generation naturally filling ministry roles.

Having broken that pattern, more effort and intentionality will be needed to re-establish it. The preparation of clergy will need to change to accommodate this growing reality. A great deal of current training equips candidates to fulfill the role of primary actor in a one-person show. That makes sense when the overwhelming number of vacancies have been for just such a setting. Although schools and colleges have attempted to address the unhealthy aspects of "Lone Ranger" clergy, in truth many graduates are entering solo ministries. With healthy part-time ministry in view, what other models and metaphors for ministry can be held up? MacDonald's "equipper", "ambassador", and "multi-staff team member" may be places to start.[2] Each of these pictures clergy as having primary roles in areas other than personal and direct ministry delivery. For instance, they might function as the trainer/mentor in some areas, as the community face of the congregation interacting in an inviting way with other aspects of the context, or as someone at the table with other (lay) team members who are equally ministers. What other skills are needed if the minister is to be the coach rather than the star of the team?

It would be an extremely positive step for the church to acknowledge that rural ministry is different from urban and suburban. It is not better, or worse, but different. For one thing, the rural pastor's life is necessarily enmeshed in the community in ways that need not pertain in the others. For example, the minister may meet their child's teacher at a school meeting, then later that night be at a Board meeting, chaired by the teacher, where the minister's salary is being decided. Still later in the week they may be sitting at that same person's kitchen table, providing pastoral care, listening to a story of historic sexual abuse. This makes the boundary issues more evident and critical.

Furthermore, as different levels of government struggle with needs that exceed revenue, the ancillary helping professions are increasingly curtailed, confronting the rural minister

"Our model for rural ministry cannot be anything at all like what urban ministry is." - Claire

with a wider range of need for which referral is not an option. For instance, mental health resources may be strained in urban/suburban contexts but virtually non-existent in rural settings. In many different aspects of life, the rural minister is not only the first, but sometimes the sole, viable contact. Is it time to consider and create rural ministry specialist streams in clergy training?

Understood in a healthy fashion, the shift to part-time is not a mere tweak in staffing levels. Nor is it a shift which the congregation might, with any luck, not notice if the clergyperson continues to don vestments and face the congregation each Sunday as ever before. It is a shift with profound implications for how the congregation organizes itself and works out its vocation. The model of *ministry-concentrate* may be welcome in some places but is killing a lot of part-time congregations and clergy. In this common pattern, clergy and congregation cooperate in a model which takes the expected practices of full-time ministry, worship leadership and preaching, administration, emergency pastoral care, regular visiting, community engagement, etc., and pares them down to what is supposedly achievable in the available number of hours. As we saw in our survey, that almost inevitably becomes inwardly focused: the minister has no time for community engagement and the congregants don't pick up the slack on those things once done by clergy. Hence the suggestions below for a different vision. In the words of an Evangelical Lutheran Church staff member:

> For a part-time pastor, really about the only thing they can do is lead Sunday morning worship and visit the sick. But in vital congregations that are having an impact on their communities and are growing, a pastor needs to be doing less visiting and more leading in engagement externally with their local community.[3]

In many locations, part-time ministry still means every Sunday worship leadership. While that may satisfy the consumer model, we have to ask whether or not that is a healthy and faithful use of highly skilled and appropriately costly resources.

As part-time calls/appointments grow in number the judicatory's work is likely to increase. As the body approving calls and appointments, there is a duty of care owed to ministry personnel. Without removing agency and freedom of choice from the pastoral charge there is room for more intense scrutiny of

"Part of it is, for me, the church that I signed on to work with for my life is not the church that is still here. The church has, in many cases, not been what I thought it was."
- Roberta

ministry settings. Under the previous model, some judicatory oversight bodies developed a deserved reputation for repeatedly approving calls/appointments to pastoral charges known to be more than usually challenging for systemic reasons. It was easier to do that then compel congregations to address significant issues. The costs of such decisions were often borne by the ministry personnel. As the number of part-time vacancies increase, is it appropriate to approve the entrance of a minister into toxic settings (marked by a refusal to acknowledge and address reality) when we know from accumulated experience that the result is likely to be negative? It can truly be asked if it is ethical to place clergy in settings where there is a fair degree of prior experience that this particular location is highly likely to damage their mental health. Is the denomination liable for placing their workers in workplaces known to be hazardous? Or, if the overseeing body feels unable to go so far as to refuse approval for such calls/appointments, can it impose a requirement for certain skills or degree of ministerial experience on the position? Our research suggests that a significant number of those entering part-time calls/appointments felt ill-prepared, inexperienced, and ill-informed about the full context. This results in a rapid turnover in clergy, which has a negative impact on congregational and ministry personnel well-being.

Another investigation worthy of consideration might plumb the true feelings of denominational and judicatory staff and representatives concerning their true feelings about part-time ministry. As we have noted, historically full-time ministry has been normative within the United Church, even though there is no official position to that effect. What messages are conveyed to clergy and congregations? Are there policies/processes in existence that hold before communities of faith the probable results of moving to part-time in the absence of a robust and widely shared renewed vision? Our research indicates that, where congregant expectations are not addressed and clergy position parameters are not articulated in conformity to a new vision, the result will be little time or energy for the tasks that lead to sustained or increased vitality. Recognizing that acclimating to the new normal may take one or two pastorates, what assistance can be provided for creative entry into an initial part-time call/appointment?

> "Acknowledge the reality, be intentional, be more strategic. Personal support for PT ministry personnel in their context. Be more honest with Candidates with respect to the potential reality. Regions intentional and persistent with realistic position descriptions. Require explorations of collaborative opportunities and partnerships. Trained and prepared ministers are a strength and an asset, not a liability, not to be compared with the value of the building!" - Workshop participant

Our research suggests that attention needs to be given to issues of language and structure. For instance, standardized reporting is an important aspect of accountability in most mainline denominations. But do the very forms of reporting give preference to certain sizes of communities of faith and trigger inappropriate feelings of inadequacy in others? It is a widely observed phenomenon that a feature of a struggling community of faith is an overwhelming governance structure that may have once been appropriate but now serves only to induce feelings of regret and unhelpful nostalgia. The community may even feel it has failed by not putting forth the full roster of congregational offices the denomination seems to anticipate. The scheduling of wider church meetings may severely restrict the participation of those in part-time calls/appointment, a loss to the broader church. The term "part-time", in some cases, carries overtones of insufficiency, lack of ability, lack of commitment, and so on. Are we able to expand the understanding of "bi-vocational" to incorporate commitments which are not employment?

> "Why isn't taking care of family an option for working part time? – What about when part-time is the choice because of illness or disability?" Workshop participant

Clergy readers may recall judicatory meetings where there was an incredible degree of negative emotion towards a minister who sought to be retained on the role of clergy in order to devote themselves to the ministry of parenthood. In the end, the person was approved and it set a precedent. We can imagine every parent at the judicatory meeting felt validated, but more importantly, language is everything and having the church recognize parenting as a vocation worthy of concentrating one's time, was key for all parents. It reminds us that family responsibilities are also given to us by God.

MacDonald's three models for pastors in part-time settings descentre the pastor and spreads responsibility and authority among the laity.[4] Edington offers a concise assessment: "A bivocational ministry is a work of the entire congregation; it is not merely a way of describing the working life of one person who happens to be ordained."[5] Bi-vocational ministry prioritizes the identification of each member's particular gifts and graces and enables them to contribute to the overall ministry of the congregation. The transformative potential of unleashing those gifts is immense.

We do not suggest that bi-vocational ministry requires less training or less demanding credentialing. Indeed, it may demand more. However, it seems that candidates for ministry leadership will need assistance to envision and reflect on a redefined role and different leadership and educational skills than they currently receive. One of our interviewees noted the absence of in-depth vocational counselling during the education process. Furthermore, bi-vocational *congregations* require an expansive understanding of Christian vocation, bridging lay and clergy, sacred and secular.

Religious educators can assist congregations in this task. A bi-vocational congregation transgresses inherited divisions between clergy and laity, sacred and secular, pastoring and mission. Each of these divisions presents an opportunity for reshaping the church and its ministry. Further research on bi-vocational congregations, building on existing research on the missional church, vital congregations, and ecclesiology is needed. Furthermore, there is a lot that white-majority, mainline congregations can learn from Christians outside their immediate demographic, many of whom have been engaged in faithful bi-vocational ministry for generations.[6]

Different possibilities

There are different ways of configuring ministry going forward. Each seeks to address a different set of circumstances with suggestions for important best practices. These should be read in conjunction with the proposals for revising judicatory processes and educational components.

Common requirements

Regardless of which model is selected there are some common elements which our research suggests should be addressed:

"The absence of administrative support is huge and very limiting." – Robert

"Administration for part-time is the same as for full-time." – Andrea

"Certainly, it remains the Community of Faith decision whether they want their clergy doing such work, but the cost of that decision must be evident, both in the hourly expense and those ministry activities which will not be done as a consequence, activities more suited to clergy training and call." – aUCC report to Region 15

1. Administrative support. Surveys, interviewees, and workshop participants were united in their insistence that appropriate administrative support is needed for part-time ministry. In too many part-time settings the clergy spend inordinate amounts of time completing routine, but time-consuming tasks (e.g., preparing worship bulletins), which means they are not doing those things for which they have been trained. It also removes one place where laity might exercise gifts. In one part-time congregation I served, one person typed the bulletin and another made the copies -- an important time savings for the clergy. While some of our interviewees referred to service bulletins, the same rationale applies to preparing Power Point, editing and posting worship videos and so on as well as a further range of important, but essentially repetitive tasks.

2. Understanding Church-size dynamics: There are many places where resources on church-size dynamics may be accessed, but it is as important for congregations to understand these features as it is for clergy. Recognizing that different sized churches operate according to different patterns and norms may shine a light on those ways of behaving that are compromising ministry.[7]

3. Peer support: Part-time ministry is lonely. The bi-vocational minister may develop connections in the other part of their life, but on the church side professional relationships are often hampered. The timing of many wider-church meetings is often such that the part-time clergy cannot attend and more casual, but important events, such as clergy cluster gatherings or retreats are often inaccessible as well. So, it is important that peer-to-peer connections for part-time clergy be emphasised and perhaps facilitated by the wider church. Perhaps an annual sponsored retreat, specifically for those in part-time ministry, addressing their concerns and leaving lots of free time for connecting.[8]

   "One of the things I've done for myself recently is I've just joined the union [Unifaith]. All of a sudden, I have colleagues, and I'm in conversation with people again. And that's good. And I have hope that I don't have to depend on the United Church." Juanita "The challenge in that too is that you're much more lonely. You don't build those collegial friendships because it's difficult to do so." – Roberta

4. Different models: While minimum salary standards are crucial as a foundational justice stone, some further work might be done to normalize part-time ministry. For instance, if the existing tables could be modified to include different sets of part-time hours, it would be a small step towards seeing this as a more common practice. Similarly, either the national or regional judicatories might develop a "menu" of options for communities of faith looking beyond the ministry-concentrate default. These options would describe an entire part-time ministry. For instance:

A model heavily weighted for worship and pastoral care hours.

A model emphasizing pastoral care and community development.

For a multi-point site, a model heavily weighted for governance meetings.

Having such a resource available not only provokes awareness of options it compels the congregation to confront and participate in appropriate priority setting. It also allows the denomination to assess accountability to the covenant of ministry while providing a boundary to "incrementalism" (the gradual adding of tasks to the ministry expectations).[9]

Different configurations: Continuing to consider different models it might be helpful, depending on the circumstances, to move away from Sunday-by-Sunday model. Several of our interviewees spoke of different practices that help keep them and the congregation fresh and engaged. Here are some questions designed to provoke reflection.

a. Does part-time mean every Sunday worship leadership? In many settings that's the assumption but is it necessary?

b. Are there greater needs in certain seasons? Perhaps there is a need for full-time work in some months. For instance, someone in a three-quarter time appointment might work full-time from September to April and congregations would exercise ministry the remaining months. Alternative arrangements can also be imagined. There may be configurations that actively assist the bi-vocational needs of that minister.

Some organizational options beyond amalgamation and cooperative ministry

Part-time congregations contemplating the future often see only amalgamation or cooperative ministry as options. These can certainly be productive if done well but it is crucial to remember that neither is an easy or simple road. An amalgamation requires time and intentionality to blend different practices, traditions and understandings of church and ministry. These factors are magnified if the merger crosses denominational lines. Done well, an amalgamation can result in a dynamic community of ministry. Many amalgamations, however, have the same result: in eighteen months the worshipping congregation is approximately the same size as the largest body entering the arrangement. We have already mentioned cooperative ministry and the cautions to be exercised entering such a joining. Here are some other options:

1. Replanting: This is a growing phenomenon that offers the hope of ongoing faithful life for a congregation that feels it has reached the end of its journey but still has some resources. A significant number of dwindling part-time congregations are in contexts where there are rich possibilities for new ministry, but the current membership lacks the energy or vision

> "If sharing with another denomination is what it takes to keep an identified space in your community, then so be it." – Andrea

to take those up. They also have some financial resources. In such a setting, a new ministry might be envisioned which, while meeting the very limited needs of the existing congregation, provides support for a new and different ministry in the same community. Such a step requires careful covenanting around the parameters of ministry because the people who participate in the new expression might be very different from current members.[10]

2. The shared ministry. A model that is growing in popularity, especially in settings where the distance between congregations of the same denomination (either geographic or theological) makes it impractical to consider merger or cooperative ministry. They are also more common in places where mainline denominations are in a theological or linguistic minority. In such a case, the minister of one tradition is authorized to preside at the sacraments and rituals of the other denomination(s) and a procedure for rotating ordered leaders between the traditions is worked out.[11]

3. The circuit or larger parish: In this model, more widely used in the United Kingdom, clergy serve a cluster of congregations, and function as trainers and mentors to lay leaders rather than as doers and producers.[12] Much of the hands-on and week-by-week ministry is conducted by lay people and the clergy are present helping to call forth and mentor existing gifts and skills. As well as requiring a different orientation to ministry this model demands different skills than are currently taught in many of our theological institutions. It does, however, offer several attractive options.

   a. Smaller communities of faith can continue as places of witness and worship beyond the point where they can afford their own clergy.

   b. There may be a larger critical mass of human resources for different forms of ministry (youth ministry, pastoral care teams, lay preaching).

   c. Skills present in one community of faith might more readily be shared between congregations than if they stood separately.

   d. For clergy, it may offer the opportunity of ministering closer to their gifts. For instance, many clergy struggle with the demands of weekly worship and preaching. They are skilled pastors, but more than occasional preaching is not a true expression of their calling. Similarly, there are gifted liturgists and preachers who can offer pastoral care but doing so constantly is an unhelpful emotional drain and some lay people may be naturally more gifted.

   e. Another version of the larger parish model that has become more common during the COVID-19 pandemic is the sharing of worship services through electronic means. A smaller congregation(s), without regular clergy, receives the worship services from a larger centre. As an ongoing model this raises the question of addressing other aspects of ministry, but it provides a potential starting place for shared work.

As the number of part-time calls/appointments continues to accelerate, proactivity on the part of judicatories and denominations can provide important positive steps. While each ministry situation is unique, there is merit in providing case studies and templates of different ways of structuring life that afford maximum opportunity for healthy, faithful, and long-term pastoral relationships.

QUESTIONS FOR DISCUSSION

1. Did any of the possibilities outlined for ministry connect with you? Which one(s)? Why?

2. What would need to change in your congregation to make one of the models work?

3. As a lay person, what special skills do you want your clergy to have? As a minister, what do you wish you had learned or learned more of in your training? How do your answers relate to part-time and/or bi-vocational ministry?

ENDNOTES

[1] MacDonald, *Part Time,* 43, citing the example of Holy Trinity Episcopal Church in Southbridge Massachusetts.

[2] MacDonald, 70ff.

[3] Quoted in MacDonald, *Part-time,*22.

[4] MacDonald, 69.

[5] Edington, *Bivocational,* Chapter Two, 6.

[6] Stephens, 11.

[7] Cf. "Congregational Size and Common Challenges" United Methodists of Arkansas, Centre for Vitality. https://docs.arumc.org/Center%20for%20Multiplying%20Disciples/Resources/Size-Theory-chart-expanded-2 .

[8] Unifaith (see sidebar text box) is a Community Chapter of Unifor, a private sector union which has, for a number of years, been seeking to organize United Church clergy. It has no official standing with the church but it is one of a couple of avenues clergy are exploring in response to feelings of isolation and a changing work environment.

[9] aUCC, "Report", 2021.

[10] Cf. Bob Smienta, "For dying congregations, a 're-plant' can offer new life' *Religion News,* January 5, 2022. Accessible at: https://religionnews.com/2022/01/05/for-dying-congregations-a-replant-can-offer-new-life/?fbclid=IwAR3gggcO9gSZP6utsn6XJGhh7xVB15S9obdUY1jJQ9oGURYGj36sepIXDk8 Accessed January 19, 2022.

[11] Cf. "Drawing from the Same Well: The St. Brigid Report," that lays out the step-by-step process for Anglican-United Church mergers: https://www.anglican.ca/faith/eir/dialogues/sbr/ Accessed January 19, 2022.

[12] Cf. Arthur Rank Centre for Rural Ministries. https://arthurrankcentre.org.uk/ Accessed January 19, 2022.

The Next Generation: Training for Part-time and Bi-vocational Ministry

Thoughts for Schools and Learning Centres

Each year, a number of people are commissioned, ordained or recognized for ministry in the United Church. The number varies but in 2020 it was 37 across the country. The Office of Vocation estimates that, on average each year, *34 more people retire than are credentialled.*[1] In 2020, twenty-six clergy were on

> *"They put us in a more vulnerable and precarious position when we can't have permanent employment and they are floating this model out there as bible."- Roberta*

"long term care" for mental health reasons (the records do not provide specific causes). Interestingly, that represented a significant drop from 2015 and 2017 (35 and 38 respectively) despite being during a pandemic. In that same year, five individuals gave notice to voluntarily leave the ministry (there are no figures regarding those who simply stopped).[2] The Barna Group, which studies faith and culture in the United States, reports that 38% of "senior pastors" have considered leaving ministry in the past year. The number jumps to 45% amongst those under 45 years of age.[3] Those interviewed cited a host of reasons that are familiar to all clergy: months of online services; tele-pastoral care; online funerals. More recently we might add tensions around the return to in-person worship, concerns about financial viability, absence of gratitude. A similar wave is likely building in Canada too. And note, these clergy are not just leaving their current calls/appointments for others (although that is disruptive enough), they are leaving ministry entirely.

> *"I want the church to know that ministry is enriched by skills that are attained in other professions."- Claire*

If the various trends identified in this study are accurate, the number of part-time calls/appointments will increase significantly. Since those who have been in ministry the shortest time appear to be the least content and feel under-prepared and -supported, is there something that can be done to better prepare and support them? We surveyed the academic heads of the various training and education institutions about where they were in terms of addressing part-time and bi-vocational ministry. Most replied. We had less success with the answers from Office of Vocation ministers and Candidacy Board chairs, therefore, we have less confidence in the broad applicability of the data we use in that aspect of this chapter.

Most of the educational institutions that replied report limited official discussion of the phenomenon and no direct curricular implications. Those conversations that are reported

"Major challenge of figuring out how to balance between the two vocations" - Marlene

have largely to do with the implications for internship.[4] Most do not engage in longer-term tracking of how and where their graduates are employed. Those programs that are located in-community are bi-vocational by design, students are working in ministry while studying, and some streams of ministry, such as diaconal ministers, have been living the part-time call/ appointment reality for much longer. Where we would invite all programs to reflect on their interaction with students is the difference between willing and reluctant bi-vocationality and how to navigate those realities. We have argued that simply having more than one job, as many part-time clergy do, is not necessarily bi-(or multi-) vocational if the individual does not see each as a calling. Further, those who are part-time unwillingly may be waiting for a full-time opportunity to arise, and those who are part-time willingly (but not bi-vocational) still need the specific skill sets identified here.

Conversations within the Candidacy process (as overseen by the Office of Vocation) are as important as action within the educational settings. The responses from those working in these formative ministries indicated that conversations about part-time and bi-vocational ministries are beginning but are largely related to ensuring candidates are aware that most

"Maintain the educational standards. . . we need high quality ministry. When we don't have high-quality ministry, it not only hurts the people in our pastoral charges, in our congregations, but it hurts the view of the whole church."- Claire

candidate appointment sites are part-time. Those reporting were unaware of the numbers of part-time positions in their jurisdictions. However, the Boards respond that most of the people under their supervision still plan to pursue full-time ministry (and feel that part-time ministry is an unfortunate reality to be dealt with for a time). The Candidacy Boards themselves have little control over where a candidate might serve as this is handled through the pastoral relations process. They do try to support candidates in their vision of their future vocation. However, it does seem to be important that a clear conversation be had with all (potential) candidates regarding evolving employment realities. How else can they be said to offer fully informed consent to credentialling for ministry?

What about students themselves? As indicated earlier, we made a limited attempt to determine the perspective of candidates themselves, querying those enrolled in the M.Div. program at Atlantic School of Theology. These students are both on-campus (i.e not employed in ministry) and summer-distance (which presumes employment in pastoral ministry). Thirty-four students replied, representing a range of years in the program and a broad geographical spectrum. Asked if anyone had spoken to them about bi-vocational or part-time ministry thus far in the candidacy program, 80% replied in the negative. The students were evenly divided in their anticipation of working full-time following ordination. When asked about their feelings regarding part-time ministry, 35.3% said this was a desirable option, 23.5% rejected it as undesirable, and the remaining 41% were open to thinking about it. 56% of the respondents indicated that they had considered bi-vocational ministry (defined in this case as "working part-time in pastoral ministry and part-time in another role"), 44% have not. Only 27% could recall bi-vocational ministry being discussed during their theological education and none could identify any training or education specific to a part-time ministry vocation. On the other hand, 79% indicated interest in training and skills towards living in part time ministry employment.

Admittedly, this is a small sample from a single school, but it does match the information received from those working in the candidacy system. Furthermore, it does incorporate students who are currently serving in pastoral ministry. It suggests that, simply because students in any stream are working in ministry

"We haven't really left behind our model of ministry from the 60s, 70s, and 80s, I think we do need a professionally trained ministry because we've got too many wackos out there" - Claire

(or other occupations) while studying, it would be misleading to consider them truly willingly bi-vocational as we are employing that term. An unknown number long for the day when they can focus fully (and full-time) on ministry. These students indicate that there has been little or no conversation with them regarding part-time ministry. This is consistent with the responses we received from educational institutions, Office of Vocation ministers, and Candidacy Board chairs.

With the growth of part-time calls/appointments and the growing acceptability and requirement of bi-vocational work, what more might be done by the church to support and strengthen future clergy. Participants in these crucial ministries (faculty, instructors, interview teams, vocations staff) might discuss amongst themselves:

1. What is your opinion of part-time calls/appointments? Do you consider them to be less than ideal? Are you, perhaps unconsciously, operating from the mindset of the full-time minister as the goal? How does that bias impact your work with students?

2. Does your school or Candidacy Board track the number of current students who anticipate part-time/bi-vocational ministry? Do you track how many graduates are actually in such ministries? Do you ever specifically poll them regarding preparation for this form of ministry?

3. What more could you do to alert candidates and students about the growing reality of part-time ministry and encourage reflection on its impact on their calling?

4. Where would a course or program segment on part-time or bi-vocational ministry fit in your curriculum? What steps would be required to make such an addition?

We suggested in an earlier chapter that the psychological and vocational self-perceptions of clergy could have a major impact on the success of a part-time ministry. Although we have not succeeded in locating academic support for this conjecture, personal experience and conversations with numerous colleagues indicate that this is a wide-spread concern. Put bluntly, the degree to which clergy become enmeshed with their clerical identity, their need to be needed, their need to be liked, their desire to be at the centre of congregational life, perfectionism, and their degree of employment uncertainty (to name a few) all militate against a thriving part-time ministry which requires clergy to advance the service of others in areas traditionally seen as reserved to the few. Unless clergy are willing, nay eager, to seek out, draw forth, and raise up the gifts of laity, a part-time ministry will not achieve its potential. The powerful myth of the omnicompetent leader in each candidate must be confronted.

Recognizing that the occurrence of part-time ministries in any location may occur across denominational lines, the importance of ecumenical training and appreciation is crucial. Smaller congregations need to see those of other traditions not as competition but as fellow workers in the same cause. If their clergy have an appreciation of other traditions, the possibility of working together on common goals (training pastoral care visitors or lay preachers for instance) increases.

As part-time clergy, our interviewees suggested several skill areas that would have been helpful for them to have addressed during their preparation for ministry. These were raised without any prompting from the interviewers. Recognizing that the educational institutions are properly independent in the shaping of curricula, it is also true that the national and regional bodies can indicate support for some aspects of the course of study leading to credentialling.[5] We also recognize that many of the curricula already have a significant number of required courses, so we are reluctant to advocate for yet further, specific courses. With some intentionality, it might be possible to include (or strengthen) these aspects within existing courses or modules.

> *"One of the joys for me is being able to say, 'sorry, we've hit the limit' or 'that's outside the range' or 'that wasn't in the priorities that we set for me.' It's put me back into the position of having more than one boss, and being able to say, 'this isn't on the job description' as we figure out what the new priorities should be." – Claire*

- Addressing the identified need for greater facility with a variety of leadership styles and modalities.
- More training in the equipping and training of church members for ministry and in "managing" them. Skills of adult education and mentoring are crucial.

- Almost unanimously they praised or asked for strong instruction on setting and maintaining healthy boundaries.
- They advocated for more/better instruction in financial literacy.
- Understanding change, change theory and change management is a crucial skill they felt they were lacking. One specifically mentioned the skills they developed during subsequent transitional/interim ministry training as being directly applicable to their part-time ministry.
- A couple of interviewees lamented the absence of strong vocational counselling and deep reflection on ministry. They noted that the models of ministry they were provided with were decades out of date from the reality on the ground. One even suggested that candidates not begin theology until they had another, marketable skill set!
- Specific foci included

  - Negotiating skills and greater awareness of different models of part-time ministry currently in practice
  - Grant writing
  - Technology
  - Time management
  - Team building

- All the interviewees stressed the need for self-care and spiritual practices to be solidly rooted.

"Perhaps need teams for the smaller, financially struggling. Can't close any more worship centres. People learning to work in teams across streams. Giving people the skills as they graduate to be able to accompany congregations into a new time. To be excited about what options there are as opposed to simply lamenting the good old days." - Catherine

There are some programmatic examples available for reference. In 2019, Earlham School of Religion launched a "Bi-Vocational Ministry Certificate", specifically inviting those with and without graduate theological degrees. The program includes topics such as: pastoral spirituality, bi-vocational mentoring, and entrepreneurial ministry.[6] "New Leaf Network" is a Canadian resource for bi- and multi-vocational ministry.[7] The extensive work and programming of the Arthur Rank Centre in England may also prove fruitful.[8] At Lancaster Seminary, Darryl Stephens is coordinating and international and interdenominational group studying the phenomenon.[9]

— — — — — —

The Road Ahead

This study began as an effort to better understand the realities of ministry that lie before graduates of ministry training. It reveals a rapidly shifting landscape where previous assumptions about the nature and scope of ministry (both in terms of practice and employment) are increasingly less valid. We have seen that part-time clergy have a range of responses to their ministry settings but are strongly united in some of the concerns they express. There are clearly significant challenges before the church as we seek to fully understand, celebrate, and utilize this gift of real ministry, provided by faithful clergy and their communities of faith.

QUESTIONS FOR DISCUSSION

1. At the end of this study, what questions about the future of ministry do you still have?
2. How can you support your minister or your ministerial colleague, especially if they are part-time?
3. If you are somewhere within the structures of the church, how has this study caused you to reimagine your approach to your important work?

ENDNOTES

[1] https://unitedchurch.sharepoint.com/sites/UnitedChurchCommons/PublicDocuments/Forms/ AllItems.aspx?id=%2Fsites%2FUnitedChurchCommons%2FPublicDocuments%2FShared%2D Publicly%2FGovernance%2FPC%2DMEPS%2FDemographic%20Report%20Presentation% 202017%2Epdf&parent=%2Fsites%2FUnitedChurchCommons%2FPublicDocuments%2FShared %2DPublicly%2FGovernance%2FPC%2DMEPS, slide 43, accessed November 25, 2021.

[2] Figures for 2020 come from private email correspondence, Office of Vocations, December 1, 2021.

[3] Melissa Florer-Bixler, "Why Pastors are Joining the Great Resignation,", *Sojourners,* November 30,2021. https://sojo.net/articles/why-pastors-are-joining-great-resignation. Accessed December 13, 2021.

[4] In the United Church, what many traditions refer to as internship is called the Supervised Ministry Education requirement, which is up to twenty-four months in a ministry placement. In-community programs often include the SME as part of the course of study.

[5] *Manual,* "Basis of Union", section 12.2.

[6] https://esr.earlham.edu/academics/certificates/bivocational/ accessed December 13, 2021. See also: Hartness M. Samushonga, "Wearing more than one hat :Preparing students for bivocational ministry is an important component of theological education," INTRUST, Autumn 2019, *www.intrust.org, pg 32,* accessed January 18, 2021.

[7] https://www.newleafnetwork.ca/multivocational .

[8] https://arthurrankcentre.org.uk/ .

[9] https://darrylwstephens.com/bivocational-and-beyond/.

Appendix 1

Study Methodology and Survey

Study Methodology
Questionnaire Design and Survey Administration

The initial draft of the questionnaire for this study was developed by the researchers,[1] with revisions subsequently made upon consultations between the researchers and Narrative Research staff members.

Prior to being finalized, the survey was pre-tested to ensure the appropriateness of the questions and response categories. The survey was available to be completed in English only on the assumption that most United Church clergy can function in that language and that this was not an official denominational project. Data collection occurred between April 16 and 23, 2021. Initial contact was made via the Office of Vocation. Two reminders were distributed after the initial invitation. The survey required approximately 22 minutes to complete, on average.

Sample Design, Selection, and Data Analysis

Any survey that is conducted is potentially subject to bias or error. When a survey is conducted with a sample of the population, there are two general classes of bias or error: sampling error, which is quantifiable, and non-sampling error, which is typically not quantifiable.

Sampling error necessarily arises from the fact that surveys are administered to only a subset of the targeted population, thus is it possible that the survey results obtained from this group of respondents is not reflective of the population as a whole.

In contrast, non-sampling error encompasses a number of different types of errors including coverage error, measurement error, non-response error, and processing error.

No measurement of sampling error can be attributed to the current study, given that the contact records used in the data collection process were derived from: an email listing of qualifying bi-vocational and part-time ministry within the Office of Vocation, together with a supplement that list, outreach to potentially additional qualifying individuals was made via social media recruitment efforts (Facebook, Twitter, etc.).

No comprehensive listing of the entirety of the target population is known to exist, and thus these survey solicitation efforts constitute a "best efforts" endeavour derived from what is believed to be recruitment from most but not all potentially qualifying personnel. Accordingly, the data collection would be deemed a non-probability sampling. As such, statistical laws prevent the application of a margin of error to the survey results.

The final data set for the survey wave was not statistically weighted, as the population parameters were not known in terms of key demographic or classification attributes such as: region, current status (part-time bi-vocational; part-time no other employment; part-time other income; years in ministry; etc.), age, and so forth.

With respect to non-sampling error, a number of steps were taken to minimize bias due to these sources. All surveys used online interviewing technology to ensure proper survey skip patterns were followed and to minimize errors due to data entry and data capture. As mentioned, the survey was pre-tested with a small sample to ensure the survey material was easily understood by respondents, and that the resultant data were being captured properly. Respondents were invited to volunteer for a longer, in-depth interview. 87% agreed! Eight individuals, characteristic of many of the broad data points, were interviewed, providing nuance and depth to the statistical learning.

Survey: Ministry Personnel Introductory page

Individuals wishing to participate in the survey were directed to a web page where they could read the details

This survey, approved by the Research Ethics Board of the Atlantic School of Theology and funded through a Seeds of Hope Grant from the United Church of Canada, is intended to provide the first comprehensive understanding of the extent of bi-vocational and part-time ministry within the United Church and some understanding of the situation and satisfaction of those in these ministries.

You are invited to participate in this survey if:

    a.   You are currently a bi-vocational or part-time minister, meaning

        a.   You are in the ordained, diaconal or DLM stream of ministry full-time and have a secondary occupation (paid or unpaid) that occupies an average of 10 hours a week or more on a consistent basis
            OR
        b.   You serve in one of those streams less than full-time
            OR
        c.   You are a candidate in one of those streams currently under appointment

AND

b. One of the following

    a. You are engaged in another activity (paid or not) at least 10 hours per week on average

    OR

    b. You are engaged in part-time ministry because no other employment opportunities are available

    OR

    c. You are economically able to engage in part-time ministry because of an alternative source of income (pension, partner's employment, etc);

Those employed in cooperative or shared ministry are encouraged to participate in the survey. This is a situation where a ministry personnel has a separate call/appointment to two or more congregations/pastoral charges which are not joined by a common governance structure.

This survey is entirely voluntary and is being conducted for the purposes of academic research. It is in no way connected to the decision-making or oversight bodies of the church. Results of the survey may be shared with church bodies, theological schools and appear in various media (journals, books, etc.)

All data collected will remain the property of the researchers and will be destroyed following the completion of the study. All data will be entirely randomized so that no identification of individual participants will be possible. This also extends to any results of follow-up conversations. A number of participants who agree will be contacted by the researchers for follow-up interviews exploring in more detail

The approximate time needed to complete survey is 15 minutes.

Those who agreed to participate were then forwarded to the actual survey

SURVEY

Thank you for participating in this survey concerning bi-vocational and part-time ministry in the United Church of Canada. Participation is voluntary and you may terminate the survey without submitting your answers at any time. You may also pause in completing the survey by clicking the "Pause" button found on every page, and then return to the survey at a later time.

To begin, please respond to the following statement

I have read and understood the purpose and parameters of this survey

Yes *[a positive response took respondents to the rest of the survey]*

No *[a negative response took respondents to the introductory page]*

Part A Basic Information

1. Which stream of ministry do you identify yourself with:

   a. Ordained
   b. Diaconal
   c. Designated Lay Ministry
   d. Candidate for ministry currently under appointment *[jump to A3]*

2. Your age at commissioning, recognition, or ordination

   a. 25-30
   b. 31-35
   c. 36-40
   d. 41-45
   e. 46-50
   f. 51-55
   g. 56-60
   h. 61-65
   i. 66+
   j. NA – in the candidacy pathway

3. Which best describes your situation (choose one):

   a. I am in a full-time call or appointment and I consider myself to be bi-vocational. I am engaged in another occupation or activity whether paid or not (employment, education, providing significant care for another, major volunteer engagement, etc).
   b. I am in a part-time call or appointment and I consider myself to be bi-vocational. I am engaged in another occupation or activity whether paid or not (employment, education, providing significant care for another, major volunteer engagement, etc). *[takes repondent to A 5]*
   c. I consider myself to be reluctantly part-time. I have been unable to secure other employment *[takes repondent to A 5]*
   d. I consider myself to be part-time. I am able to work part-time because of other income (e.g. pension, partner income, etc.) *[takes repondent to A 5]*

4. As someone who identifies as bi-vocational currently, were you employed in your current non-pastoral-ministry vocation prior to commissioning, recognition, ordination?

   a. Yes
   b. No

5. How many years have you served in ministry since your ordination, commissioning or recognition or as a candidate for ministry? (Please count any partial years as full years for this question. E.g., 3 years and 2 months should be entered as 4 years)

    a. 0-3
    b. 4-6
    c. 7-10
    d. 11-15
    e. 16-20
    f. 21-25
    g. 25-30
    h. 31+

6. Are you currently in a (choose one)

    a. Call
    b. Appointment

7.

    a. My call or appointment is full-time *[Takes respondent to E14]*
    b. If your call or appointment is designated as part-time, please select the number of hours listed on the call/appointment form. (Note: if you are serving a co-operative ministry please answer only for the largest call/appointment. If they are equal, choose one. You will be asked about others later in the survey)
    c. 7-10
    d. 11-16
    e. 17-20
    f. 21-25
    g. 26-30
    h. 31-35
    i. 36-39

8. Are you the only ministry personnel employed by your community of faith?

    a. Yes
    b. No *[a negative response took the respondent to questions related to team ministry Part C]*

Part B Solo Ministry

1. As the only ministry personnel are you responsible for:

   a. 1 congregation
   b. 2 congregations
   c. 3 congregations
   d. 4 congregations
   e. 5 or more congregations

2. Counting only the primary service of praise and worship, how many services do you conduct in an average week?

   a. One service
   b. Two services
   c. Three services
   d. Four or more services

3. As the sole ministry personnel, which of the following areas of ministry are your regular, primary focus (choose all that apply):

   a. Preaching and worship leadership (including planning and preparation)
   b. Emergency Pastoral Care (funerals, serious illness or crisis)
   c. Regular Pastoral Care (visiting members in home or hospital)
   d. Administration (meetings, etc.)
   e. Christian Education for adults
   f. Christian education for children and youth
   g. Visioning and/or strategic planning

4. Have you discussed your ministry priorities with the governing body?

   a. Yes
   b. No

5. Do you feel the terms of your call/appointment provide you with enough time to accomplish most of the tasks of ministry?

   All the time
   Most of the time
   Some of the time
   Rarely
   Never

6. Do you regularly find yourself working more than the number of hours in your call/ or appointment

   a. Yes *If yes respondent is taken to B7]*
   b. No *If no, respondent is taken to D6]*

7. On a regular basis, how many hours a week do you work beyond those named in your call/appointment

   a. 1-3 hours
   b. 4-6 hours
   c. 7-10 hours
   d. 11-13 hours
   e. 14-15 hours
   f. More than 15 hours

8. Can you identify a reason(s) why you regularly work the extra hours? (Choose all that apply)

   a. There's too much work to do in the allotted time.
   b. I have a special project that is a passion for me.
   c. I see the extra hours as a form of discipleship.
   d. I'm bored and need something to do.
   e. I feel pressure from the congregation/pastoral charge.
   f. I have difficulty saying "no"

Part C Team Ministry

1. As part of a ministry team, how many others are employed with you in ministry/ pastoral tasks?

   a. 1 other
   b. 2 others
   c. 3 others
   d. 4 others
   e. 5 or more

2. How many of those in question C1 are full-time

   a. 1
   b. 2
   c. 3
   d. 4 or more

3. How many of those in question C1 are part-time

   a. 1
   b. 2
   c. 3
   d. 4 or more

4. Are you in a specialized or focused area of ministry?

   a. Yes
   b. No

5. If "yes" would you define the focus of your ministry as (choose all the apply)

   a. Children, Youth and Families
   b. Worship
   c. Preaching
   d. Christian Education for Adults
   e. Community Outreach
   f. Pastoral Care

Part D Factors in Ministry

6. As a person in a part-time call/appointment, do you feel that the congregation(s) you serve understand the constraints of your position

   a. Yes
   b. No

7. Have you sought and received support in making choices about time use and priorities?

   a. Yes
   b. No

8. If yes, what sources (choose all that apply):

    a. Colleagues in your community of faith
    b. Ministry and Personnel Committee
    c. Governing Body
    d. Lay Leaders
    e. Part-time colleagues in other communities of faith
    f. Friends and/or mentors

9. How comfortable do you feel with the time-use and priority choices you have made?

    a. Very comfortable
    b. Somewhat comfortable
    c. Okay I guess
    d. Uncomfortable
    e. Very uncomfortable

10. Are you involved in the wider life of the church (Region, National, Office of Vocation, etc)?

    a. Yes
    b. No

11. Does your congregation see your involvement with the wider church as part of your call or appointment?

    a. Yes. A certain amount of time is included in the terms of call/appointment
    b. No. Any involvement is on my own time.

Part E The Other Part of Your Life

In answering these questions please focus on the part of your life not covered by the previous sections.

1. All things being equal I would prefer to be employed full-time in one pastoral charge/community of faith.

    a. Yes
    b. No *[takes respondent to E4]*

2. I am not employed full-time because (choose all the apply):

    a. I am unable to relocate geographically
    b. Shortage of full-time call/appointment opportunities
    c. Family responsibilities *[takes respondent to E6]*
    d. Health limitations

3. If a full-time vacancy was declared I would apply for it

    a. Yes
        a. If it was within driving distance of my current location
        b. Anywhere in the Region
        c. Anywhere in the country

    b. No. I am unable to undertake full-time work at this time due to other responsibilities or limitations.

4. I am happy not to work full-time at this point because (choose the answer that most applies to you):

    a. I have sufficient income (pension or other source) *[takes respondent to E5]*
    b. I have sufficient income (partner employment) *[takes respondent to E8]*
    c. I enjoy the freedom to care for family *[Takes respondent to E6]*
    d. I enjoy the freedom to pursue other endeavours (paid or unpaid) *[Takes respondent to E7]*
        I feel equally called to my non-ministry vocation *[Takes respondent to E7]*

5. I am receiving pension income: *[Answer takes to E8]*

    a. From the United Church or another denomination or church-related employer;
    b. From another source.

6. I am an important or primary caregiver to *[Answer takes to E8]*

    a. a. my children
    b. b. older relatives
    c. c. spouse/partner

7. I have other paid employment (please indicate which is the most accurate)

    a. Under call or appointment in the church (please specify)
        a. Another pastoral charge (a cooperative ministry) *[Go to E Supp 1]*
        b. Another pastoral charge (a specialized focus) *[Go to E Supp 1]*
        c. Another denomination *[Go to E Supp1]*
        d. A role at the Regional or National level

e.   A chaplaincy or church-related teaching position

b.   In the church but not a call/appointment

   a.   Another pastoral charge (a cooperative ministry)
   b.   Another pastoral charge (a specialized focus)
   c.   Another denomination
   d.   A role at the Regional or National level
   e.   A chaplaincy or church-related teaching position

c.   As a solo entrepreneur
d.   As an employee of government (public service, health service, education, military, police, etc.)
e.   As an employee of a company or corporation
f.   As an employee of a non-for-profit and/or social agency

8. Working part-time suits me because

   a.   I can exercise other talents
   b.   I enjoy the freedom and flexibility
   c.   I meet other people
   d.   I have opportunities for evangelism
   e.   I earn more than in my church role

9. I consider the work I do outside my principal church call/appointment to be a genuine vocation or calling

   a.   Yes
   b.   No

10. The primary challenges in my current life are:

   a.   Balancing responsibilities
      f.   Employment uncertainty
      g.   Explaining to people why I'm not a full-time minister
      h.   Explaining to people why I'm a minister
      i.   Dealing with congregational expectations
      j.   e Other:

11. What are the primary resources that support you in your bi-vocational ministry

12. What do you wish your congregation understood about your employment situation:

13. What do you wish the wider church understood about your current vocation:

14. Do you feel that bi-vocational ministry is valued and supported by the following:

Region

a. Yes

b. No

Regional Minister

a. Yes

b. No

Office of Vocation

a. Yes

b. No

What could the wider church do to better support you as a bi-vocational minister:

15. We are interested in why you have added a second component when you are already employed full-time. Remembering that we are referring to an activity (paid or unpaid) that occupies a minimum of ten hours a week.

Were you employed in your current non-pastoral-ministry vocation prior to commissioning, recognition, ordination?

a. Yes

b. No

Please indicate which general field best characterizes your second employment:

a. In the church (please specify)
   Another pastoral charge (a cooperative ministry)
   Another pastoral charge (a specialized focus)
   A role at the Regional or National level
   A chaplaincy or church-related teaching position

b. As a solo entrepreneur

c. As an employee of government (public service, health service, education, military, police, etc.)

d. As an employee of a company or corporation

e. As a volunteer of a not for profit and/or social agency

f. As a care-giver in your family

g. Other

You undertake this extra role because (please indicate all that apply)

a. I feel a sense of call or vocation to this work
b. The pay and benefits from my ministry employment are insufficient to meet my needs
c. I enjoy the extra income
d. I want to give back to society/church
e. Family responsibility
f. It is an important outlet for my gifts and skills

Part E Supp 1 *(in multiple church calls/appointments)*

1. If you hold a second call or appointment is it

a. Solo ministry *[Go to Part E Supp 2]*
b. Team Ministry *Go to Part E Supp 3]*

Part E Supp 2 *[2nd appointment/call – solo]*

2. Please select the number of hours listed on the call/appointment form.

a. 6 or less
b. 7-10
c. 11-16
d. 17-20
e. 20 or more

3. As the only ministry personnel are you responsible for:

a. 1 congregation
b. More than 1 congregation

4. Counting only the primary service of praise and worship in your second call/appointment, how many services do you conduct in an average week?

a. One service
b. Two or more services

5. As the sole ministry personnel, which of the following areas of ministry are your regular, primary focus (choose all that apply):

    a. Preaching and worship leadership (including planning and preparation)
    b. Emergency Pastoral Care (funerals, serious illness or crisis)
    c. Regular Pastoral Care (visiting members in home or hospital)
    d. Administration (meetings, etc.)
    e. Christian Education for adults
    f. Christian education for children and youth
    g. Visioning and/or strategic planning

6. Have you discussed your ministry priorities with the governing body?

    a. Yes
    b. No

7. Do you feel the terms of your call/appointment provide you with enough time to accomplish most of the tasks of ministry?

    a. All the time
    b. Most of the time
    c. Some of the time
    d. Rarely
    e. Never

8. Do you regularly find yourself working more than the number of hours in your call/ or appointment

    a. Yes *If yes go to next question*
    b. No *If no, go to D6*

9. On a regular basis, how many hours a week do you work beyond those named in your call/appointment

    a. 1-3 hours
    b. 4-6 hours
    c. 7-10 hours

10. Can you identify a reason(s) why you regularly work the extra hours? (Choose all that apply)

    a.   There's too much work to do in the allotted time.
    b.   I have a special project that is a passion for me.
    c.   I see the extra hours as a form of discipleship.
    d.   I'm bored and need something to do.
    e.   I feel pressure from the congregation/pastoral charge
    f.   I have difficulty saying "no

11. Do you hold a third call or appointment

    a.   Yes *Go to 10*
    b.   No *Go to Part F*

12. Is this 3rd call/appointment in

    a.   Solo Ministry *Go to E Supp 4*
    b.   Team Ministry *Go to E Supp 5*

Part E Supp 3 *[2nd appointment/call – team]*

1. As part of a ministry team, how many others are employed with you in ministry/pastoral tasks?

    a.   1 other
    b.   2 others
    c.   3 others
    d.   4 others
    e.   5 or more

2. How many of those in question 1 are full-time

    a.   1
    b.   2
    c.   3
    d.   4 or more

3. How many of those in question 1 are part-time

    a.   1
    b.   2
    c.   3
    d.   4 or more

4. Are you in a specialized or focused area of ministry?

    a. Yes
    b. No

5. If "yes" would you define the focus of your ministry as (choose all the apply)

    Children, Youth and Families

    a. Worship
    b. Preaching
    c. Christian Education for Adults
    d. Community Outreach
    e. Pastoral Care

    Do you hold a third call or appointment?

    a. Yes *Go to next*
    b. No *Go to Part F*

    Is this 3rd call/appointment in

    a. Solo Ministry *Go to E Supp 4*
    b. Team Ministry *Go to E Supp 5*

Part E Supp 4 -*3rd Part time appointment call – solo*

1. Please select the number of hours listed on the call/appointment form for your third call/appointment.

    a. 6 or less
    b. 7-10
    c. 11-16

2. As the only ministry personnel are you responsible for:

    a. 1 congregation
    b. More than 1 congregation

3. Counting only the primary service of praise and worship in your third call/appointment, how many services do you conduct in an average week?

    a. One service
    b. Two or more services

4. As the sole ministry personnel, which of the following areas of ministry are your regular, primary focus (choose all that apply):

    a. Preaching and worship leadership (including planning and preparation)
    b. Emergency Pastoral Care (funerals, serious illness or crisis)
    c. Regular Pastoral Care (visiting members in home or hospital)
    d. Administration (meetings, etc.)
    e. Christian Education for adults
    f. Christian education for children and youth
    g. Visioning and/or strategic planning

5. Do you feel the terms of your call/appointment provide you with enough time to accomplish most of the tasks of ministry?

    a. All the time
    b. Most of the time
    c. Some of the time
    d. Rarely
    e. Never

6. Do you regularly find yourself working more than the number of hours in your call/ or appointment

    a. Yes *If yes go to 7*
    b. No *If no, go to Part F*

7. On a regular basis, how many hours a week do you work beyond those named in your call/appointment

    a. 1-3 hours
    b. 4-6 hours
    c. 7-10 hours

8. Can you identify a reason(s) why you regularly work the extra hours? (Choose all that apply)

    a. There's too much work to do in the allotted time.
    b. I have a special project that is a passion for me.
    c. I see the extra hours as a form of discipleship.
    d. I'm bored and need something to do.
    e. I feel pressure from the congregation/pastoral charge
    f. I have difficulty saying "no

GO TO F

Part E Supp 5 *[3rd appointment/call – team]*

1. As part of a ministry team, how many others are employed with you in ministry/pastoral tasks?

   a. 1 other
   b. 2 others
   c. 3 others
   d. 4 others
   e. 5 or more

2. 2 How many of those in question 1 are full-time

   a. 1
   b. 2
   c. 3
   d. 4 or more

3. 3 How many of those in question 1 are part-time

   a. 1
   b. 2
   c. 3
   d. 4 or more

4. 4 Are you in a specialized or focused area of ministry?

   a. Yes
   b. No

5. 5 If "yes" would you define the focus of your ministry as (choose all the apply)

   a. Children, Youth and Families
   b. Worship
   c. Preaching
   d. Christian Education for Adults
   e. Community Outreach
   f. Pastoral Care

GO TO PART F

Part F

How others perceive us may have a significant impact on our ability to exercise ministry and leadership. It may also affect the sorts of ministries to which we are called and appointed. The following questions seek to probe those correlations. If this is an uncomfortable area for you, please indicate. You will be taken to the final questions of the survey and your answers will be entered. *Click here to end survey – Takes to G*

These questions ask about your understanding of how *others* perceive *you*

1. Do most people see you as:

    a. Caucasian
    b. African-Canadian
    c. Asian
    d. First Nations
    e. Other

2. Do you think most of your congregation(s) see you as:

    a. Younger than your age
    b. Older than your age
    c. Roughly your own age

3. Do you feel the leadership in your congregation(s) treat you as:

    a. Younger than your age
    b. Older than your age
    c. Roughly your own age

4. Do you feel that generally your congregation and its leadership, feel you are

    a. Fully committed to ministry
    b. Partially committed to ministry but distracted by your other employment
    c. Minimally committed to ministry because you are distracted by your other employment

Part G

A few demographic questions to conclude.

1. Do you identify as (click all that apply)

    a. Male
    b. Female
    c. Gay or Lesbian
    d. Transgender
    e. Two-Spirited
    f. Prefer not to say

2. Your age

    a. 25-30
    b. 31-35
    c. 36-40
    d. 41-45
    e. 46-50
    f. 51-55
    g. 56-60
    h. 61-65
    i. 66-70
    j. 70+
    k. Prefer not to say

3. Marital status:

    Married
    Never married
    Divorced
    Separated
    Prefer not to say

4. Number of dependents (whether dwelling with you or not)

    1
    2
    3
    4
    5+

5. Location of residence

    a. Alberta/BC
    b. Manitoba/Saskatchewan
    c. Northern Ontario
    d. Southern Ontario
    e. Quebec
    f. New Brunswick/ Nova Scotia/ Prince Edward Island
    g. Yukon/Iqualuit/ NWT
    h. Bermuda
    i. Newfoundland and Labrador

In a second stage of our research, we will conduct more in-depth interviews with certain survey respondents to develop a fuller picture of bi-vocational and part-time ministry. If you would be willing to be interviewed, in an entirely confidential manner, please indicate below. Unfortunately, available resources will only allow us to interview a limited number of volunteer participants. Only those selected for interviewing will be contacted but we are very grateful to all who wish to give further assistance.

I am willing to receive an invitation to a further interview. I am aware that, at a later date, I can decline to be interviewed even if I agree now.

There will be a check box here. If participants click the box it will open a dialogue box requesting:

Your name:_____

Email address_____

Confirm email address_____

ENDNOTES

[1] The questions were approved by the Ethics Review Board, Atlantic School of Theology.

Appendix 2

Church structures: who does what?

Different traditions have different structures. In order to assist the transferring of insights from one church to another, we present the following chart and invite readers to translate to their own context.

National:

a. The General Council, meets regularly every three years; equal numbers of clergy and laity, elected from the Regions. Overall policy setting and denominational direction.

b. The General Council Executive, chosen for particular skills and diversity, conducts church business between meetings of the General Council

c. The Office of Vocation, is a body of the General Council responsible for the standards of training for clergy, their admission, oversight and discipline. The work is done through regionally deployed staff and volunteer committees. One of these, the Candidacy Board, active in every Region, has the oversight and approval of candidates for ministry.

Regional

The denomination is divided into sixteen geographic regions of approximately equal numbers of members. As a result, because of population concentration and dispersion, some are quite large. The Regional Council of clergy and laity meets annually and has oversight and direction of numerous educational, financial, social justice and other work within its bounds. Critical to this study is the pastoral relations function, explained below.

Local

The local expression of the church is the Community of Faith or Congregation (the terms are used interchangeably). The Community of Faith may be a single preaching point or a gathering of two or more preaching points under a shared governing body (a "multi-point" charge.

Bibliography

Bentley, Kristen Plinke. "Perspectives of Bi-Vocational Ministry: Emerging Themes in Bi-Vocational Ministry Research at Lexington Theological Seminary." *Lexington Theological Quarterly* 48 no. 3-4 (Fall and Winter 2018). 115-31, http://www.lextheo.edu/wp-content/ uploads/2019/10/j-4-Perspectives-of-Bi-Vocational-Ministry.pdf

Bibby, Reginald W. *Beyond the Gods and Back: Religion's Demise and Rise and Why It Matters*. Lethbridge: Canada Project Books, 2014.

Bickers, Dennis W. *The Work of the Bivocational Minister*. Valley Forge: Judson Press, 2007.

Carroll, Jackson W. *God's Potters: Pastoral Leadership and the Shaping of Congregations*. Grand Rapids: Eerdmans, 2006.

Christian Reformed Church in North America. *Study of Bivocationality Task Force*, October 2020, https://www.faithaliveresources.org/Products/830135/study-of-bivocationality-task-force.aspx.

Edington, Mark D. W. *Bivocational: Returning to the Roots of Ministry*. New York: Church Publishing, 2018. http://www.bivocational.church.

Florer-Bixler, Melissa, "Why Pastors are Joining the Great Resignation." *Sojourners Magazine*, November 30, 2021. https://sojo.net/articles/ why-pastors-are-joining-great-resignation.

Forum for World Evangelization, "The Local Church in Mission." *Lausanne Occasional Paper* no. 39. (Fall 2004): https://www.lausanne.org/content/lop/ local-church-mission-lop-39#cpb.

Global Connections, *The Challenge of Tentmaking, Serving God through One's Profession and Business Overseas*, 2008, https://www.globalconnections.org.uk/sites/newgc.localhost/files/papers/The%20Challenge%20of%20Tentmaking.pdf.

Jones K (2017) 'Who am I? Bi-vocational ministers and pastoral identity', unpublished paper, Atlantic School of Theology, available at https://library2.smu.ca/handle/01/27050

Kirkpatrick, Nathan. "It's Time to Recalibrate Expectations for Clergy." *Faith and Leadership*, August 5, 2014. https://faithandleadership.com/its-time-recalibrate-expectations-clergy.

MacDonald, G. Jeffrey. *Part-Time is Plenty: Thriving without Full-Time Clergy*. Louisville: Westminster John Knox, 2020.

Niebuhr, H. Richard, and Daniel D. Williams. *The Ministry in Historical Perspectives*. New York: Harper and Brothers, 1956.

Noll, Mark. *A History of Christianity in the United States and Canada*. Grand Rapids: Eerdmans, 1992.

Reimer, Sam and Rick Hiemstra. "The Rise of Part-time Employment in Canadian Christian Churches." *Studies in Religion* Volume 43, no. 3 (2015): 356-377.

Samushonga, Hartness M. "Wearing more than one hat: Preparing students for bivocational ministry is an important component of theological education." *INTRUST*, Autumn 2019. 32. www.intrust.org.

Samushonga, Hartness M. "On Bivocational Ministry-focused Training in British Theological Schools: Dialoguing with British Theological Educationalists." *Practical Theology* 13 (2020): 385-399.

Stephens, Darryl. "Healing Congregations: A Corrective to the Metrics of Congregational Vitality." *Witness: Journal of the Academy for Evangelism in Theological Education* 34 (2020).

Stephens, Darryl W. "Bivocational Ministry as the Congregation's Curriculum." *Religions* 12, no. 1 (January 15, 2021): 56. https://doi.org/10.3390/rel12010056.

United Church of Canada. *The Manual*. Multiple editions. Toronto: United Church of Canada.

United Church of Canada, *Minimum Salaries & Reimbursements for Ministry Personnel*, 2021, https://united-church.ca/sites/default/files/2021-salary-schedule-ministry-personnel.pdf.

United Church of Canada, *Ministry Leadership to Meet the Needs of the Church in the 2020s*, November 2021, https://unitedchurch.sharepoint.com/:w:/r/sites/UnitedChurchCommons/_layouts/15/Doc.aspx?sourcedoc=%7B-557F3F8D-17BF-4AE5-A749-DD4448D0C0B8%7D&file=Ministry%20Leadership%20to%20Meet%20the%20Needs%20of%20the%20Church%20in%20the%202020s%20Report%20FINAL.docx&action=default&mobileredirect=true.

Watson, James W., and Santos, Narry F, "Tentmaking: Creative Mission Opportunities within a Secularizing Canadian Society", in Santos and Naylor (eds.), *Mission and Evangelism in a Secularizing World: Academy, Agency, and Assembly Perspectives from Canada*, Evangelical Missiological Society Monograph Series 2. (Eugene: Pickwick, 2019) pp. 131–48.

Watson JW et al., *The Canadian Multivocational Ministry Project Research Report*, Report, The Canadian Multivocational Ministry Project, (Toronto 2020). Available at: https://static1.squarespace.com/static/5dcdba9db0a67a6df5d6d739/t/5ec8093204e37806001cb60a/1590167859876/2020+Research+Report+Canadian+Multivocational+Project.pdf

Printed in Canada